'DAT LITTLE CAJUN COOKBOOK
BY REMY

A Certified Product Of Louisiana

RELCO PUBLISHING

COVER PHOTO: RUSS GANSER
COVER DESIGN: SHARON FREEMAN & SUSIE
PAGE DESIGN: SUSIE AYO
COPY EDITOR: GILLY JAUNET

1

© Copyright 1993 by

RELCO
PUBLISHING

P.O. Box 3942
Lafayette, La 70502-3942

ISBN 0-9632197-1-5   Library of Congress Catalog Card Number 93-87066

CHEF REMY has published this cookbook in order to make available one of the styles of delicious Cajun cuisine that can be prepared with familiar condiments and ingredients. Information on those ingredients that are not available in your area can be obtained by writing CHEF REMY at address listed above.

All recipes have been tested, but differences in meat types, oven and stove temperature, elevation, cooking utensils, and availability of necessary ingredients must be considered in all instances of success and failure. Every attempt has been made to keep the recipes simple, yet complete.

✶ DEDICATION ✶

THIS BOOK IS DEDICATED FIRST AND FOREMOST
TO OUR LORD JESUS CHRIST
WITH WHOM ALL THINGS ARE POSSIBLE.

IT IS ALSO DEDICATED
TO THE PEOPLE OF SOUTH LOUISIANA.

'DAT LITTLE CAJUN COOKBOOK

FOREWORD

Because of the great demand for Cajun cooking recipes I have decided to provide this series of more specialized and compact versions of the traditional cookbook: "THE MINI COOKBOOK."

As you flip through this book, you will find that there are plenty of recipes to cook in an easy-to-follow format. Don't be surprised at the size, because as we all know…good things come in small packages.

✺ Brief Cajun History ✺

In the early 17th century, a group of French peasants settled in Acadia, Nova Scotia. Later, in the mid 18th century, Britain acquired Canada, forcing the loyal French settlers to leave. Most of these settlers managed to migrate to south Louisiana, where their descendants still live. These descendants are called Cajuns. The most popular explanation of the name is that the local Indians could not pronounce Acadians properly, hence the term "Cajuns."

Cajun cooking was influenced by many sources, in fact, many of the same sources as the "Creole" influences. I am frequently asked, "What is the difference between Cajun and Creole cooking?" This is a difficult question to answer because of the many similarities. Especially now, the styles of living and cooking are very similar. The main difference in cooking styles is that the first Cajuns did most of their cooking in one pot, while the Creoles had more facilities for cooking and more money available for more elegant and

(Continues)

diverse styles. Because of a greater Spanish influence, Creoles used more red sauces in their cooking and less dark roux. These differences in style still exist today in many respects, but the styles are getting closer and closer together all the time.

Food is more than just a means to survive here in Louisiana. It has become an integral part of the lifestyle and culture. It is said that most people eat to live, but in Louisiana, we live to eat. When you combine that with the rich heritage, and the great music, what you get is a people with a joy for life. You get a party!

❧ Terms to Understand ❧

Bisque   A thick spicy soup, usually with a cream base and some meat or seafood.

Blackened   To fry a seasoned, coated piece of meat or fish in butter on a very high temperature until black in color.

Cajun Trinity   Chopped onion, bell pepper and celery.

Caramelize   To sauté onion, bell pepper and celery in butter until moisture is gone and vegetables begin to brown.

7

(Continues)

ETOUFFEÉ   To smother with onions and other vegetables. (Usually bell pepper and celery)

FRICASSEE   To sauté meat or fowl in butter and then cook (or braise) in a seasoned liquid.

GRILLADES   Thinly sliced strips of meat (usually pork) that are pan fried.

GUMBO   Basically a Cajun soup that has a roux base.

JAMBALAYA   Everything mixed together and cooked in one pot, with rice and stock, and cooked until rice has absorbed almost all liquid.

PANNÉ   To fry a breaded or floured meat in a small amount of oil on high heat. This is usually done in a cast iron skillet but any skillet will do.

ROULADE — Rolled meat or poultry.

ROUX — Roux is simply a cooked mixture of oil or butter and flour. There are three basic rouxs for cooking. The white roux is used in white sauces and for simple thickening. The tight (or medium roux) is a paper bag colored mixture used for thickening and flavor. Finally there is a dark roux that is used primarily for color and flavor. (Instructions to follow)

STOCK — Water that has been enriched by boiling parts of meat and/or vegetables until the essence of the parts has become a part of the liquid. Always strain stocks and skim fat to assure a pure and lo-cal source of flavor and nutrition.

Cajun Meats

Andouille	Usually a large diameter sausage that is made up of pork and seasoning that is smoked until completely cooked. Used in gumbos and jambalayas.
Smoked Sausage	Cajun smoked sausage is similar to most smoked sausages except that it is usually more highly seasoned and smoked with a variety of wood from hickory to pecan or oak.
Tasso	Tasso is a very lean ½" thick sliced pork that is highly seasoned and smoked to perfection. Tasso can be used as a meat source or as a type of seasoning to enhance vegetables or sauces.

∽ About the Author ∾

Chef Remy was born, raised in, and is a current resident of south Louisiana. His cooking experience goes back to age 9 when he first took an interest in cooking. His mother is a great cook of Italian heritage and would spend hours preparing the daily offerings.

He began to get serious about cooking when he was just out of high school but was not able to go into the field until much later in life. While living among the Cajun people in Lafourche Parish, he began to write his first cookbook, "I Want 'Dat Cajun Cookbook." He has since been able to pursue his dream of cooking professionally while cooking in and managing a restaurant. He has also cooked in two other restaurants, while cooking and coordinating for two catering services. Chef Remy enjoys cooking at festivals and gift shows whenever possible. He was named Grand Champion of the Ville Platte, La., smoked meat

(Continues)

festival in June of 1993. His commitment to continued education and excellence has placed him among the truly committed Louisiana cooks.

"Raising your level of cooking in the Louisiana professional cooking community is so important because of the fierce competition and because of the level of quality cuisine that has been achieved here. The standards of cooking in the world are being set in south Louisiana, and to be learning and working here is truly an honor", says CHEF REMY.

His cooking comes from the heart, which is an attitude that exists in the Cajun lifestyle. His desire to share his recipes with you is culminated in this series of mini cookbooks. If you are a collector, then these books are great to make a part of your collection. If you just like to cook, then you must certainly add the passion of Cajun cooking to your repertoire.

∽ THE ROUX ∾

WHITE ROUX The white roux is simply butter or margarine and flour. This is the base of white sauces, cream sauces and white or sawmill gravy. It is made by melting butter and adding flour and blending completely. In this case, there is usually more butter than flour. I recommend for every tablespoon of butter, you add 1½ tablespoon of flour.

TIGHT ROUX The tight (light brown or medium) roux is used primarily to thicken, although it is flavorful as well. This is made with either butter or oil and flour (although I recommend butter). Equal parts of butter and flour are used to achieve this roux. Melt butter (or heat oil) and add flour. Whisk together and continue on medium high heat until mixture thickens and becomes a paper bag brown color.

13

(Continues)

DARK ROUX   The dark roux is possibly the most used roux in Cajun cooking. There are several opinions about the color of a dark roux. I use a very dark colored roux (about the color of dark chocolate) and have a definite style of preparing it. Most say to mix equal amounts of oil (**Do Not** use butter, and use an oil that can stand up to high heat, i.e. peanut oil or canola), and flour, but as you become familiar with the process, you can increase the flour-to-oil proportion by about 20%.

HOW TO COMPLETE THE DARK ROUX

It is important that you understand the importance of a successfully completed roux. Since it is an integral part of a lot of Cajun recipes, you must not scorch or burn the roux. When you first begin to make roux, you will experience a very distinctive smell. In fact, the completed roux, will have a slightly burned smell. If you follow the instructions to the letter, you will not burn the roux. You must use patience in this process. If you are not patient, you will surely burn the roux or will not complete the desired color. Once you have mastered the process, this smell will become pleasant to you and all in your household, because the smell means something good is coming from the kitchen.

Heat oil to slightly hot. Add flour and blend with the utensil of your choice (most people say a wooden spoon; some use a metal spatula; I use a wire whisk). YOU MUST WHISK OR STIR THE MIXTURE, CONSTANTLY SCRAPING THE BOTTOM AND EDGES, UNTIL ROUX IS COMPLETED! Keep on high heat until flour begins to brown. When the oil begins to smoke, you must reduce heat to medium or medium high (depending on your skill) and continue to whisk or stir until the roux gets to a dark brown color. At this stage you can do a couple of things. You can remove the roux from heat and stir until the roux

15

(CONTINUES)

is cool enough to stop darkening. If you choose this process, you must remove the roux **before** you reach the desired color. It will progress to a darker color because of the heat that is retained in the oil. The other option is to remove from heat when the roux is almost the color you want, then add chopped fresh onion to the hot roux and stir until the onions stop steaming. (CAUTION! THE STEAM FROM THE ONIONS WILL BURN YOU IF YOU ARE NOT CAREFUL.) I use the latter method.

⚘ Appetizer's ⚘

Fried Mushrooms 17

Cream Cheese Stuffed Mushrooms 18

Cream Cheese Sauce 20

Popcorn Shrimp 22

Fromage Sauce 23

Cajun Drumettes 24

Boudin Balls 26

Oysters Rockefeller 28

Cajun Meat Pies 30

Spinach Dip to Die For 32

Cajun Deviled Eggs 34

Cajun Cocktail Sauce 35

Marinated Crab Claws 36

Hot Crawfish Dip 38

Cajun Fried Chicken Bits 40

Easy Rotel Cheese Nachos 42

∾ Food Quantities for 25 Servings ∾

Rolls	4 doz
Bread	50 slices or 3 1 lb. loaves
Butter	½ lb
Mayonnaise	1 cup
Mixed Filling for Sandwiches	
meat, eggs, fish	1½ quarts
Mixed Filling, Sweet, fruit	1 quart
Jams & Preserves	1½ lb
Crackers	1½ lb
Cheese (2 oz. per serving)	3 lb
Soup	1½ gal
Salad Dressings	1 pt
Potato Salad	4½ quarts
Scalloped Potatoes	4½ quarts or 1-12x20" pan
Mashed Potatoes	9 lb
Spaghetti	1¼ gal
Baked Beans	¾ gal
Jello Salad	¾ gallon
Canned Vegetables	1 #10 can
Lettuce (for salads)	4 heads
Carrots, 3 oz. or ½ cup	6¼ lb
Tomatoes	3-5 lb
Wieners, beef	6½ lbs
Hamburger	9 lbs
Turkey or Chicken	13 lbs
Fish, large, whole	13 lbs
Fish, filets or steaks	7½ lbs
Watermelon	37½ lbs
Fruit Cup (½ cup per serving)	3 quart
Cake	1-10x12 sheet cake
	1½ 10" layer cake
Ice Cream, Brick	3¼ quarts
Bulk	2¼ quarts
Coffee	½ lb and 1½ gal. water
Tea	1/12 lb and 1½ gal. water
Lemonade	10 to 15 lemons, 1½ gal. water

✄ Fried Mushrooms ✄

1 LB	SMALL MUSHROOMS	½ TSP	GARLIC POWDER
2 CUPS	ALL PURPOSE FLOUR	1	EGG
1 CUP	CORN FLOUR (FISH FRY)	¾ CUP	MILK
1 TSP	SALT	1 TBSP	CREOLE MUSTARD
1 TSP	WHITE PEPPER		OIL FOR FRYING
½ TSP	CAYENNE PEPPER		

Wash mushrooms and set aside on a paper towel to dry. Mix all purpose flour, corn flour, salt, white pepper, cayenne pepper and garlic powder in a bowl. In another bowl, completely blend egg, milk and creole mustard. Add ¼ cup dry mixture to egg mixture, and whisk until totally blended. Heat oil until approximately 350°F. When oil is hot, dip mushrooms into egg mixture, then into dry mixture. Shake excess and fry until brown.

✍ CREAM CHEESE STUFFED MUSHROOMS ✍

1 LB	LARGE MUSHROOMS	2 TBSP	PARSLEY FLAKES
¼ LB	BUTTER	2 TBSP	WHOLE SWEET BASIL, DRIED
1 CUP	ONIONS, FINELY CHOPPED	1 TBSP	SALT
½ CUP	BELL PEPPER, FINELY CHOPPED	2 TSP	PEPPER
¼ CUP	CELERY, FINELY CHOPPED	8 OZ	CREAM CHEESE
2 TBSP	GARLIC, MINCED	2½ CUPS	SEASONED BREAD CRUMBS
2 TBSP	ALL PURPOSE FLOUR	½ CUP	PARMESAN CHEESE
2 CUPS	HEAVY CREAM		

Wash mushrooms, then pop out stems; reserve caps. Finely chop mushroom stems and reserve. In a 10" skillet heat butter on medium high heat until melted. Add onions, bell pepper, celery, chopped mushroom stems and garlic. Sauté until onion begin to clear; add flour and stir in well. When flour is totally blended, add heavy cream and whisk until all flour is dissolved. Add parsley flakes, basil, salt, pepper and continue to whisk until mixture begins to thicken. Add cream cheese in small pieces and whisk until totally blended. Remove from heat.

Next, add bread crumbs a little at a time until mixture is thick enough to handle (you should have some bread crumbs left over to top the stuffing) and allow to cool for 1 hour at room temperature. After cooling, generously spoon stuffing mixture in each mushroom cap. Roll the mushroom top in remaining bread crumbs until coated and sprinkle with parmesan cheese. Place mushrooms in baking pan, and pour 1 cup water around mushrooms. Cover with foil and bake at 350°F for 30 minutes or until brown. Makes 20-25.

✦ Cream Cheese Sauce ✦

¼ LB	BUTTER
2 TSP	SALT
2 TSP	BLACK PEPPER
2 TBSP	ALL PURPOSE FLOUR
2 CUPS	HALF AND HALF OR HEAVY CREAM
1 TBSP	WHOLE SWEET BASIL
1 TBSP	PARSLEY, DRIED
8 OZ	CREAM CHEESE
2 TSP	WORCESTERSHIRE SAUCE

In a 1-quart saucepan melt butter on high heat. Add salt, black pepper and flour, then whisk until blended. Add half and half (or heavy cream) and whisk until blended. Keeping on high heat, continue to whisk until mixture begins to thicken. Add whole sweet basil and parsley and continue to whisk until thick. Reduce heat to low, cover and simmer 15 minutes, stirring occasionally. Next, cut cream cheese into 6-8 pieces. Return pot to high heat, add cream cheese (a couple of pieces at a time) to pot and whisk until totally blended. Remove from heat, add worcestershire sauce and whisk in until blended. Use hot or cold as a dip or topping for fish, stuffed mushrooms, fried foods or vegetables or use your imagination.

～ Popcorn Shrimp ～

1 LB	SHRIMP, PEELED (90-110's)	1 TSP	CAYENNE PEPPER
4 CUPS	CORN FLOUR	1 TSP	GARLIC POWDER
1 TBSP	SALT	1 QT	OIL FOR FRYING
1 TBSP	PEPPER	½ CUP	YELLOW MUSTARD

Make sure shrimp are peeled, washed and drained well. Pat shrimp in paper towels to dry. Reserve shrimp in a bowl. Next, mix corn flour, salt, pepper cayenne pepper, and garlic powder until totally blended. In a 2½-quart pot, heat 1 quart oil to 360°F .

Add yellow mustard to the reserved shrimp and mix well. Dredge the shrimp through the corn flour mixture until well coated.

Shake off excess, drop in hot oil and fry until golden brown.

❧ Fromage Sauce ❧

¼ LB	Butter	2 OZ	Sharp Cheddar Cheese
1 TBSP	All Purpose Flour	2 OZ	Cream Cheese
½ TSP	Salt	2 OZ	Swiss Cheese
1 TSP	Cayenne Pepper	2 OZ	Monterey Jack Cheese
3 CUPS	Milk	2 OZ	Colby Cheese
2 OZ	American Cheese	2 OZ	Garlic Cheese

In a 2-quart saucepan, melt butter on high heat. Add all purpose flour, salt and cayenne pepper and whisk until blended. Add milk and whisk until blended. Keep on high heat and continue to whisk mixture until it begins to bubble rapidly. Add cheeses, one cheese at a time, blending each cheese with the whisk and blending totally until all cheeses are incorporated. Serve hot as a dip or as topping for vegetables. Serves 6.

∽ Cajun Drumettes ∾

24	CHICKEN WINGS	½ CUP	MAYONNAISE
1 TSP	SALT	2 TBSP	SOUR CREAM
1 TBSP	PEPPER	3 CUP	ALL PURPOSE FLOUR
2 TBSP	CREOLE MUSTARD	1 CUP	CORN FLOUR
1 TBSP	WORCESTERSHIRE SAUCE	2 TBSP	CAJUN SEASONING (PAGE 128)
2 CUPS	BUTTERMILK	½ TSP	CREAM OF TARTAR
1 TBSP	PARSLEY FLAKES		OIL FOR FRYING

Note: If you would like to make your own Cajun seasoning, refer to the "Seasonings" section of this cookbook.

First, cut chicken wings in three. The end portion or tip of the wing should be discarded. The top part (or drumette) is the main part of the recipe, but the center portion of the wing is great to fry as well. Wash the chicken parts well, pat dry and sprinkle with salt and pepper. Next, mix flour, corn flour and Cajun seasoning together. In a separate bowl, mix mayonnaise, sour cream mix, creole mustard, worcestershire sauce, buttermilk, cream of tarter and parsley flakes until completely blended (a wire whisk works best).

Heat oil to 360°F for frying. Dredge the chicken pieces in the dry mix until lightly coated (be sure to shake off all excess). Dip chicken parts into the wet mixture until richly coated and then into the dry mixture again until there are no wet spots on the chicken. Carefully drop the coated pieces into the hot oil and fry until golden brown. This should take about 10-12 minutes. Serve hot or cold. Great addition to any party layout.

❧ Boudin Balls ❧

2 TBSP	PORK FAT		2 TSP	CAYENNE PEPPER
2 TBSP	ALL PURPOSE FLOUR		2 TBSP	DRY PARSLEY, DRIED
1 CUP	YELLOW ONION,		2 TBSP	PAPRIKA
	FINELY CHOPPED		2-3 TBSP	GARLIC, MINCED
½ CUP	PORK FAT		2 CUPS	CHICKEN OR PORK STOCK
1 LB	GROUND PORK		8 CUPS	COOKED RICE, LONG GRAIN
7 OZ	GROUND PORK LIVER			SEASONED BREAD CRUMBS
1 TBSP	SALT		1 QUART	PEANUT OIL, FOR FRYING

In a 10 inch skillet, stir together over heat 2 tbsp pork fat and flour (make a roux). Stir with flat spatula until dark brown. Remove from heat, add onion and stir until onions stop sizzling. Remove from skillet and reserve. Next, heat remaining pork fat, add ground pork and brown until broken. Add pork liver, stir in well and continue to brown 5 minutes. Add salt, cayenne pepper, parsley, paprika and garlic. Stir well, and simmer on medium low heat, covered, for 20 minutes, stirring occasionally. Add reserved roux and stir in well. Add chicken stock and stir well. Cover and simmer 10 more minutes. Remove from heat and allow to cool. If you have a processor with a mixing blade, add cooked rice and meat mixture and blend completely, or mix well in a bowl until totally blended. Form into 2 inch balls, and roll around in bread crumbs until totally covered. Heat oil in a 2 quart pot until 360°F. Fry until golden brown. Makes 25 balls. Freezes well.

❧ Oysters Rockefeller ❧

2 DOZ	OYSTERS IN THE SHELL	1 TBSP	BELL PEPPER, FINELY CHOPPED
10 OZ	FROZEN CHOPPED SPINACH	1 TSP	BLACK PEPPER
¼ LB	BUTTER	½ TSP	CAYENNE
1 CUP	WATERCRESS, CHOPPED	½ TSP	FLOUR
¼ CUP	GREEN ONION, MINCED	1 TSP	BASIL
¼ CUP	PARSLEY, CHOPPED	½ CUP	HEAVY CREAM
½ TSP	WHOLE THYME		

First you must open or shuck the oysters. If you don't have an oyster knife, then it is easy to open commercially cultivated oysters with a common can opener, (some call them church keys).

Locate the hinge of the oyster. It will appear as an overlapping end of the oyster. Place the pointed end of the can opener in the hinge as far as possible. Pry to break the hinge.

When oyster opens, slide the knife along the top (flat) shell to cut the top muscle clean. The top shell will fall off. Carefully cut the bottom muscle of the oyster to free the oyster from the shell. Save the bottom curved part of the oyster shell. Clean and scrub shell. Reserve the oysters in their juice until you need them.

Next, drain spinach very well. In a heavy saucepan melt butter over medium heat. Add spinach, watercress, green onion, parsley, bell pepper and simmer until onion is clear, stirring frequently, for 5 minutes. Add pepper, cayenne, flour, basil, heavy cream, thyme and cook until thickened.

Remove from heat and let cool. Dry off oysters. Place oysters (one to each shell) into cleaned shells. Spoon mixture over each oyster and bake in a preheated 400°F oven for 10-15 minutes until brown and bubbly. If oysters are not in the shell, you can make or purchase foil shells to take the place of a real shell. Also, pepper sauce is great on top!

∽ Cajun Meat Pies ∞

STEP ONE, THE PASTRY:
IF YOU DON'T HAVE TIME TO MAKE THE RECIPE, PREMADE EGG ROLL WRAPPERS WORK WELL, BUT
YOUR OWN HOMEMADE PASTRY IS MUCH BETTER.

2½ CUPS	ALL PURPOSE FLOUR	1 TSP	SALT
1 TSP	SUGAR	½ CUP	MILK
½ CUP	SHORTENING		

In a bowl combine flour, sugar and salt. Pour into a food processor with the blade attachment.
With processor on, add shortening in a small chunks. Mix well until flour and shortening
form pea sized balls, then add milk a little at a time until dough forms together. Scrape
dough out on floured sheet and roll out to 1/16 inch thick. Cut out 4 inch circles. Lightly flour
both sides and reserve.

Step Two, Ground Beef Filling:

3 TBSP	BACON FAT	1 TSP	CAYENNE
½ CUP	BELL PEPPER	1 TSP	ALLSPICE, GROUND
½ CUP	YELLOW ONION	1 TSP	SALT
½ CUP	GREEN ONION	½ TSP	BLACK PEPPER
1 TBSP	GARLIC, MINCED	½ LB	LEAN GROUND BEEF
2 TBSP	PARSLEY FLAKES	2 SMALL	EGGS, BEATEN (TO SEAL PIES)

Finely chop bell pepper, yellow onion and green onion. Melt fat and add everything except beef and egg and cook for 5 minutes. Add beef and brown. Drain in a colander and let cool. Place 2 tbsp filling in center of pastry circle. Moisten edges of circle with egg, fold over to form a half circle and press to seal (a fork works well). Deep fry at 350°F until brown. Drain on paper towel. Serve.

Note: You can bake in a preheated 350°F oven for about 8 minutes, turn over and bake other side 8 minutes or until brown. Makes about 25 4-inch pies.

๑ Spinach Dip to Die For ๑

¼ LB	BUTTER	1 TSP	SALT
1 CUP	ONION, MINCED	1 TSP	BLACK PEPPER
½ CUP	BELL PEPPER, MINCED	1 TBSP	CAJUN SEASONING (PAGE 128)
¼ CUP	CELERY, MINCED	2 TBSP	ALL PURPOSE FLOUR
2 TBSP	GARLIC, MINCED	2 CUPS	HEAVY CREAM
1 TBSP	PARSLEY, DRIED	10 OZ	FROZEN CHOPPED SPINACH,
2 TBSP	BASIL, DRIED		THAWED AND DRAINED
1 TSP	WHOLE THYME	2 DASHES	PEPPER SAUCE

In a 2-quart saucepan, melt butter on high heat. When melted and bubbly, add onion, bell pepper, celery and garlic. Sauté for 5 minutes, or until onions are clear. Add parsley, basil, thyme, salt, pepper and Cajun seasoning. Stir well. Add flour and stir in until blended. Add heavy cream and whisk until mixture begins to thicken. Cover, reduce heat to low and simmer for 15 minutes, stirring frequently. Add spinach to mixture and stir in well. Cover and continue to simmer another 15 minutes. Remove from heat, stir in pepper sauce, and allow to cool at room temperature. For cold dip, it is recommended that you refrigerate for 6-12 hours. You can serve hot straight out the pot. Cool to room temperature before refrigeration. Freezes well. Serves 10 at a party with other entrees.

‿ Cajun Deviled Eggs ‿

12	Jumbo Eggs	2 tbsp	Creole Mustard
⅔ cup	Mayonnaise	1 tsp	Yellow Mustard
1 tbsp	Parsley, dried	1 tsp	Worcestershire Sauce
1 tsp	Salt	¼ cup	Dill Pickles
1 tsp	White Pepper	3 dashes	Pepper Sauce
½ tsp	Cayenne Pepper	6	Pimento Stuffed Olives
1 tsp	Garlic, crushed		

Put eggs in a 2-quart pot, cover with cold water to 2 inches above eggs. Boil 20 minutes until hard boiled. Pour out hot water and immerse eggs in very cold water. Peel eggs, cut in half, reserve whites. Add yellows to food processor along with all other ingredients except olives. Blend well. Fill egg whites to cover entire top of egg half. Slice olives in half and top each egg. Makes 24 Deviled Eggs.

⚘ Cajun Cocktail Sauce ⚘

1 CUP	KETCHUP
2 TBSP	CREOLE MUSTARD
2	LEMONS, JUICED
½ CUP	ONION, VERY FINELY MINCED
1 TBSP	GARLIC, VERY FINELY MINCED
3 TBSP	FRESH PARSLEY, MINCED
2 TBSP	WORCESTERSHIRE SAUCE
	SALT AND PEPPER TO TASTE
10 DROPS	PEPPER SAUCE
1 TBSP	HORSERADISH SAUCE

Mix all ingredients together. Chill for at least 2-4 hours at least. Have plenty for seafood boil. It goes fast.

∽ Marinated Crab Claws ∾

When counting crab claws, I suggest you consider the ones I refer to are South Louisiana blue crabs. Even the largest claws are only 1½ to 2 inches long once they have been cracked. This recipe will work with other species of eatable crab, just adjust for size.

24	Cracked Crab Claws	½ tsp	Salt
¼ cup	Olive Oil	½ tsp	Pepper
½ cup	Red Wine Vinegar	1 tsp	Garlic Powder
1 tbsp	Bell Pepper, finely minced	¼ cup	Onion, finely minced
2 tbsp	White Wine Worcestershire Sauce	2 tsp	Pepper Sauce

Place crab claws in a plastic sealable container (preferably a container designed for marinating foods). Next, in a food processor, pour in olive oil and turn processor to the fixed on position. Slowly add the vinegar. Add all other ingredients, one at a time, until all are added. Continue to process 30 seconds more until totally blended and creamy looking. Pour mixture over crab claws, cover and seal. Shake the container until marinade covers all claws. Refrigerate for 24 hours. Serve cold over a bed of lettuce. Serves 4-6.

❧ Hot Crawfish Dip ❧

¼ LB	BUTTER	2 TSP	PEPPER SAUCE
1 CUP	ONION, MINCED	2 TBSP	WHOLE SWEET BASIL
½ CUP	BELL PEPPER, MINCED	2 TBSP	PARSLEY, DRIED
¼ CUP	CELERY, MINCED	3 TBSP	ALL PURPOSE FLOUR
2 TBSP	GARLIC, MINCED	3 CUPS	HEAVY CREAM
2 TSP	CAJUN SEASONING (PAGE 128)	8 OZ	CREAM CHEESE
1 TSP	SALT	2 TSP	WORCESTERSHIRE SAUCE
1 TSP	BLACK PEPPER	1 LB	CRAWFISH TAILS, PEELED

In a 2-quart saucepan melt butter on high heat. When butter is hot, add onion, bell pepper, celery and garlic. Simmer for 10 minutes on high heat, stirring frequently. Next, add Cajun seasoning, salt, black pepper, pepper sauce, whole sweet basil and dry parsley. Stir well, continuing to simmer for another 3 minutes. Add all purpose flour, and stir until totally blended. Continue to stir on high heat for another minute. Add heavy cream, and whisk until mixture begins to thicken. Reduce heat to low, cover and simmer 5 minutes. Meanwhile, cut cream cheese into 8 pieces and add to mixture, stirring until completely blended. Add worcestershire sauce and whisk in well. Add crawfish (including all fat and juices), and stir well. Cover and simmer on low heat for 10 minutes, or until mixture is 160°F. Serve hot in a heated chafing dish, with crackers or patty pastries. Do not reuse or freeze. Serves 30-40 at a party.

❧ Cajun Fried Chicken Bits ❧

6	Chicken Breasts, boneless
2 cups	All Purpose Flour
2 cups	Corn Flour
1 tbsp	Cajun Seasoning (page 128)
1 tsp	Salt
1 tbsp	Black Pepper
2 cups	Buttermilk
¼ cup	Mayonnaise
1 tsp	Garlic, granulated
1	Egg
	oil for frying, suggest vegetable or peanut oil

Clean and pound chicken breasts. Cut breasts into ¾ inch squares, pat dry and reserve. In one bowl combine flour, corn flour and Cajun seasoning, reserve. In another bowl combine salt, black pepper and buttermilk. Blend together well. Add mayonnaise and blend until smooth. Add granulated garlic and egg, and blend until completely mixed. From the first bowl of dry ingredients, remove ½ cup of mixture and add to buttermilk mixture. Blend with a whisk until totally mixed. Heat oil to 350°F. Add chicken to dry mixture and remove, shaking off excess. Then add pieces, a few at a time, to buttermilk mixture, allowing excess to drip off chicken, then dip into the dry mixture. Mix in well with fingers until chicken is coated. Again, shake off excess, then carefully drop into hot oil to fry. Do not stir until chicken pieces have been in oil for at least 1 minute. Stir well and fry until golden brown. Remove and drain. Serves 4-6.

❧ Easy Rotel Cheese Nachos ❧

1 LB	VELVEETA STYLE CHEESE
1 CAN (10 OZ)	DICED ROTEL TOMATOES
3 DASHES	PEPPER SAUCE, OPTIONAL

ON THE STOVE • In a 1-quart double boiler, melt cheese until completely melted and hot. Add rotel tomatoes to melted cheese and stir. Bring back to bubbly hot. Stir in 3 dashes pepper sauce. Serve over nacho chips or use as a dip. Serves 6.

IN THE MICROWAVE • Cut cheese into 1 inch squares and place into covered microwave dish. Heat on high for 2 minutes, stir. Rotate the dish and repeat the process. Add diced rotel tomatoes and stir well. Heat on medium for 4 minutes, stir well. Add pepper sauce, serve as above.

ꙮ Soups and Gumbo ꙮ

Stocks...43

Chicken and Corn Soup 46

Creamy Corn Bisque 48

Okra Gumbo 50

Chicken and Sausage Gumbo 52

White Bean Soup 55

Oyster Soup 56

Crab Bisque..57

Artichoke Bisque...58

Seafood Gumbo..60

Size of Pans and Baking Dishes

Common Kitchen Pans to use as Casseroles when the Recipe calls for:

4 cup Baking Dish:
9-inch pie plate
8x1¼-inch layer cake pan
7⅜x3⅝x2¼-inch loaf pan

6 cup Baking Dish:
8 or 9x1½ inch layer cake pan
10-inch pie plate
8½x3⅝x2⅝-inch loaf pan

8 cup Baking Dish:
8x8x2-inch square pan
11x7x1½-inch baking pan
9x5x3-inch loaf pan

10 cup Baking Dish:
9x9x2-inch square pan
11¾x7½x1¾-inch baking pan
15x10x1-inch jelly-roll pan

12 cup Baking Dish and over:
13½x8½x2-inch glass baking pan, 12 cups
13x9x2-inch metal baking pan, 15 cups
14x10½x2½-inch roasting pan, 19 cups

When you are planning to cook almost anything that requires water as an ingredient, you can immediately improve your dish by substituting stock in place of that water. Stocks are nutritious and flavorful. When you use stock instead of water, you remove the neutrality of the liquid base and replace it with flavor. Your recipe will have a richness that plain water cannot provide.

Stocks are easy to prepare. Since you are using that which you normally discard, the cost of making stock is limited to the energy it takes to make it. Instead of throwing those bones, shells, vegetables, skeletons or innards away, you can put them in a pot, cover with water and boil until the essence of those ingredients is released to the water, thus producing stock.

One simple example of a stock is perhaps the most versatile stock to keep. Chicken stock is easy to prepare. When you get a whole chicken, you receive a packet of eatable organs. Not everyone eats these parts of the chicken, but even if you don't eat them, they make good stock. In addition, if you take the time to cut the chicken, you have pieces and skin left over that you usually discard. I like to debone the pieces, which leaves all the bones to use as well. Place all of the bones, skin and organs, including the neck, in a pot and cover with water. Bring to a rapid boil. Cover and simmer on medium low heat for 2 hours. Strain completely, then place all stock in a container. Chill for 3 hours. Remove the fat at the top of the container and discard.

What you have left is a nutritious, flavorful stock that you can use in virtually any recipe, especially gravy. If you are not going to use the stock immediately, then return the fat-less stock to a pot and reduce to one-half of volume and freeze in ice trays. Remove cubes from ice trays and store in a zip lock type freezer bag in the freezer. This will allow you to use just the amount of stock needed.

When you peel shrimp, boil the heads and peeling to make a great seafood stock. Don't throw away those fish heads and bones. Use them to produce a great fish stock. Instead of throwing out all the unused parts of the vegetables you prepare, use them to produce a nutritious soup stock. Cooking with stock will improve almost anything you cook.

∽ CHICKEN AND CORN SOUP ∾

1	WHOLE CHICKEN FRYER	2 TSP	SALT
2 TBSP	VEGETABLE OIL	1 TBSP	BLACK PEPPER
1 CUP	ONION, CHOPPED	1¼ CUP	DICED ROTEL TOMATO
½ CUP	BELL PEPPER, CHOPPED	4 CUPS	WHOLE KERNEL YELLOW CORN
¼ CUP	CELERY, MINCED	2 QUARTS	CHICKEN STOCK
2 TBSP	GARLIC, MINCED	3 TBSP	CORN STARCH DISSOLVED IN
2 TBSP	PARSLEY FLAKES	¼ CUP	WATER
2 TBSP	WHOLE SWEET BASIL		

In a 4-quart pot, boil chicken in enough water to cover until completely cooked (about 45 minutes). Chicken should be falling apart. Remove chicken to large bowl and allow to cool.

Strain stock. Return to pot and boil until reduced to about 2 quarts. Reserve. Next, in a 4-quart pot, heat oil to hot. Add onion, bell pepper, celery, garlic, parsley and basil to hot oil and sauté until onions begin to wilt. Add salt, pepper and rotel tomato, and simmer on medium heat for 10 minutes. Add corn and stir well. Add reserved chicken stock and bring to boil. Reduce heat to low, cover and simmer for 30 minutes.

While mixture is simmering, pick all the meat from the boiled chicken. When mixture has simmered for 30 minutes, add chicken meat to pot and stir. Add cornstarch mixture to pot and stir well. Cover and remove from heat. Serve.

∽ CREAMY CORN BISQUE ∾

¼ LB	BUTTER
3 TBSP	ALLPURPOSE FLOUR
1 TSP	SALT
2 TSP	BLACK PEPPER
1 QUART	MILK OR HEAVY CREAM
2 TBSP	OLIVE OIL
1 CUP	ONION, CHOPPED
¼ CUP	CELERY, MINCED
1 CUP	CHICKEN STOCK, CONCENTRATED
½ TSP	CAYENNE PEPPER
4 CUPS	WHOLE KERNEL CORN

In a 2-quart saucepan, melt butter on high heat. Add flour, salt and black pepper, and whisk until bubbly. Add milk or heavy cream, and whisk until totally blended. Keeping on high heat, continue to whisk until mixture thickens (about 10 minutes). Remove from heat and reserve.

In a 4-quart saucepan, heat olive oil on high heat. Add onion and celery, and sauté until onions begin to brown, stirring frequently. Add chicken stock, cayenne pepper and bring to boil. Add corn and stir well. Return to boil. Add reserved cream mixture and blend well. Reduce heat to low, cover and simmer for 25 minutes, stirring occasionally. Serves 10.

❧ OKRA GUMBO ❧

"GUMBO" ACTUALLY IS AN AFRICAN WORD MEANING "OKRA." OKRA SEED WAS SMUGGLED TO AMERICA IN THE HAIR OF SLAVES. THE TERM WAS ADOPTED BY SOUTH LOUISIANA PEOPLE AFTER TASTING THE DISH COOKED BY THOSE SLAVES. THE ACTUAL DISH CALLED OKRA GUMBO WAS NOT THE SOUPY DISH WE HAVE COME TO LOVE. OKRA WAS COOKED SLOWLY IN A COVERED POT TO DE-SLIME THE VEGETABLE, THEN SERVED AS IS OR OVER RICE. THIS RECIPE IS MY VERSION WHAT IS NOW PERCEIVED AS OKRA GUMBO.

¾ CUP	VEGETABLE OIL	1 TBSP	SALT
1¼ CUP	FLOUR	1 TBSP	PEPPER
1 CUP	ONION	½ TSP	CAYENNE PEPPER
½ CUP	BELL PEPPER	1 LB	OKRA
¼ CUP	CELERY	2 QUARTS	CHICKEN STOCK

1 TBSP	GARLIC	1 LB	PORK SMOKED SAUSAGE
2 TBSP	OLIVE OIL		COOKED RICE
¼ CUP	PARSLEY		

First, chop all vegetables and slice sausage. Next heat oil on high heat until hot. Add flour and whisk until blended. Continue to whisk on high heat until color begins to brown and roux begins to smoke. Quickly reduce heat to medium and continue to whisk, scraping sides and bottom completely until dark brown. Remove from heat and add onion, bell pepper, celery and garlic. Stir in well (beware of steam). Reserve.

In a large pot heat olive oil. Add parsley, salt, pepper, cayenne and okra, and simmer on medium high until okra is limp (20 minutes). Add chicken stock, and bring to boil. Add roux, blend well and boil on medium heat for 30 minutes. Add sausage and boil 20 minutes. Serve over rice.

Chicken and Sausage Gumbo

10 LB	Chicken Leg and Thigh Quarters
6 quarts	Water
2 cups	Vegetable Oil
2½ cups	All Purpose Flour
4 cups	Onion, chopped
2 cups	Bell Pepper, chopped
1 cup	Celery, chopped
½ cup	Fresh Parsley, chopped
¼ cup	Garlic, minced
2 tbsp	Salt
1 tbsp	Black Pepper
1 tsp	Cayenne Pepper

1 TSP	PEPPER SAUCE
½ TSP	GROUND THYME
3 LB	CAJUN SMOKED SAUSAGE

In a 10-quart pot, cover chicken pieces with at least 6 quarts water. Be sure to cover chicken at least 3 inches above chicken. Bring to boil on high heat and cook for 1½ hours. Remove chicken to bowl to cool. Strain stock completely. Skim off all fat and return to heat to boil. Make sure there is at least 5-quarts of liquid.

In a 8-quart pot, heat oil to hot. Add flour and whisk until blended. Continue to whisk flour mixture, scraping the sides and bottom constantly and consistently without stopping, until mixture begins to smoke and turns brown. Quickly reduce heat to medium and continue to whisk until roux is a dark brown (about the color of dark chocolate).

As soon as dark color is achieved, remove from heat. Add onion and stir well (beware of steam) until sizzling stops. Return to medium heat. Slowly add 5 quarts of the reserved

(CONTINUES)

stock, blending with a whisk until all stock is blended. Liquid should be brown but thin. Add 1 quart of water and blend well. Return heat to high and bring to boil. Add bell pepper, celery, parsley, garlic, salt, pepper, cayenne pepper, pepper sauce and thyme. Stir until well blended. Reduce heat just enough to maintain a moderate boil. Boil for 1 hour. While gumbo is boiling, pick all meat from chicken and reserve, also slice sausage to desired thickness.

Next add all sausage and stir well. Continue to boil for 30 more minutes. Reduce heat to low. Cover and simmer for 10 minutes. Uncover and skim off all oil. Return to high heat and simmer another 10 minutes. Add picked chicken and stir well. Cover, remove from heat, and let stand for 20 minutes. Serve over cooked rice. Serves 20. Freezes well.

❦ WHITE BEAN SOUP ❧

1 LB	NAVY BEANS		2 TBSP	PARSLEY
2 QUARTS	CHICKEN STOCK		2 TSP	SALT
¾ CUP	ONIONS		1 TSP	BLACK PEPPER
¼ CUP	CELERY		5 DASHES	PEPPER SAUCE
1 TBSP	GARLIC, MINCED		1 LB	SMOKED SAUSAGE

In a 4-quart pot, cover beans with water (about 2 quarts). Stir well, and let stand for 2 hours. Next, chop vegetables and slice sausage to desired thickness. Pour out water and cover beans with at least 2 quarts chicken stock. Place on high heat and bring to boil for 30 minutes. Add remaining ingredients except for sausage. Stir well. Boil on high for 1 hour, stirring occasionally, adding liquid to maintain desired texture. Add sausage and simmer for 45 minutes covered. Serves 10-12.

✎ Oyster Soup ✐

2 PINTS	OYSTERS IN LIQUOR	2 TBSP	WHOLE THYME
1/2 TSP	SAGE, DRIED	1 CUP	ONION, CHOPPED
1/2 TSP	ROSEMARY	1/4 CUP	FRESH CHOPPED PARSLEY
1 TSP	CAYENNE PEPPER	1/4 CUP	WHOLE SWEET BASIL
1 TSP	PEPPER SAUCE	1 QUART	WATER

Remove oysters from liquor. Strain liquor and place in a 4-quart pot and bring to boil. Add all other ingredients except water and reserved oysters. Bring to boil, then reduce heat to maintain moderate boil. Boil for 1 hour. Next, add water and bring back to boil for 15 minutes. Add oysters and reduce heat to simmer. Cover and simmer 15 minutes. Salt to taste. Serve.

❧ CRAB BISQUE ❧

¼ LB	BUTTER	1 CUP	SEAFOOD STOCK
2 TBSP	FLOUR	3 CUPS	HALF & HALF CREAM
1 TSP	SALT	8 OZ	CREAM CHEESE
1 TBSP	BLACK PEPPER	1 LB	LUMP CRAB MEAT
1 TSP	WHOLE THYME	½ CUP	CHOPPED GREEN ONION
1 TBSP	WHOLE BASIL		

In a 2-quart pot heat butter on high heat. Add flour and whisk until flour is blended and bubbly. Whisk in salt, pepper, thyme and basil. Add seafood stock and whisk until totally blended. Mixture will be thick. Add half and half cream and whisk until totally blended. Reduce heat to low, cover and simmer 10 minutes. Return to high heat and blend in cream cheese. Simmer on low for 10 minutes. Add crab meat and stir gently. Top with green onion and serve. Serves 8.

∾ Artichoke Bisque ∾

3 cups	Marinated Artichoke Hearts,
	drained, reserve liquid
¼ lb	Butter
2 tbsp	Flour
½ cup	Onion, chopped
½ cup	Green Onion, chopped
¼ cup	Fresh Parsley, chopped
1 tsp	Salt
2 tsp	White Pepper
3 cups	Heavy Cream
1 cup	Artichoke Juice

| ¼ TSP | PEPPER SAUCE |
| 1 CUP | GRATED PARMESAN CHEESE |

Place all but 4 of the artichoke hearts in a food processor and process until finely chopped, reserve. Cut remaining hearts in half and reserve. In a 3-quart pot melt butter on high heat. Add flour and whisk until totally blended. Continue to whisk until flour just begins to brown. Immediately add onion, green onion, parsley, salt, white pepper, and whisk in well. Add heavy cream and blend in. Add artichoke liquid and blend well. Add all reserved artichoke to pot and stir in well. Add pepper sauce and stir well. Bring to bubble, reduce heat, cover and simmer for 30 minutes. Add parmesan cheese and stir in well. Remove from heat, cover and let stand for 10 minutes. Serves 8.

✑ Seafood Gumbo ✑

2 LB	SHRIMP, MEDIUM, UNPEELED WITH HEADS
10	GUMBO CRABS, SMALL
4 DOZ.	OYSTERS & LIQUOR
2 LB	CRAWFISH, BOILED
1¾ CUPS	VEGETABLE OIL
2 CUPS	ALL PURPOSE FLOUR
2 CUPS	ONION, CHOPPED
	ALL RESERVED SEAFOOD STOCK & enough WATER TO MAKE 8 QUARTS
1 CUP	BELL PEPPER, CHOPPED
½ CUP	CELERY, CHOPPED
¼ CUP	PARSLEY, CHOPPED

¼ CUP	GARLIC, minced
3 TBSP	SALT
1 TBSP	BLACK PEPPER
1 TSP	CAYENNE PEPPER
1 TBSP	WHOLE THYME
1 CUP	GREEN ONION, chopped

Peel shrimp and remove heads. Reserve shrimp. Place peeling and heads in 6-quart pot with 4 quarts water. Strain oysters and add liquor to pot. Put on high heat and boil for 1 hour. Strain completely and discard peeling and heads. Reserve stock.

In a 12-quart pot heat oil to hot. Add flour and whisk until blended. Continue to whisk until flour turns a dark brown (see roux instruction on pages 13 & 14).

As soon as roux turns dark brown, remove from heat and add chopped onion; stir in well. Return to high heat and begin to slowly add stock, stirring and

(CONTINUES)

blending. Add all of the stock plus enough water to make 8 quarts. Add bell pepper, celery, parsley, garlic, salt, black pepper, cayenne pepper and thyme. Stir well and bring to boil. Boil for 1 hour on medium heat. Add salt to taste. Add cleaned, broken gumbo crabs; stir. Boil on medium heat for 15 minutes. Add shrimp and continue to boil for another 10 minutes. Add boiled crawfish and boil another 5 minutes. Top with chopped green onion (or save green onion to top each individual serving). Serve over hot rice. Serves a bunch.

❧ Poultry ❧

Chicken Sausage Jambalaya 63

Chicken Sauce Piquant..66

Apple Pepper Chicken 68

Blackened Duck...69

Chicken Etouffee' 70

Stuffed Baked Chicken...72

ເ POULTRY ROASTING GUIDE ຄ

Type of Poultry	Ready-To-Cook Weight	Oven Temperature	Approximate Total Roasting Time
Turkey	6 TO 8 LBS	325°	2½ TO 3 HOURS
	8 TO 12 LBS	325°	3 TO 3½ HOURS
	12 TO 16 LBS	325°	3½ TO 4 HOURS
	16 TO 20 LBS	325°	4 TO 4½ HOURS
	20 TO 24 LBS	300°	5 TO 6 HOURS
Chicken, Unstuffed	2 TO 2½ LBS	400°	1 TO 1½ HOURS
	2½ TO 4 LBS	400°	1½ TO 2½ HOURS
	4 TO 8 LBS	325°	3 TO 5 HOURS
Duck, Unstuffed	3 TO 5 LBS	325°	2½ TO 3 HOURS

NOTE: SMALL CHICKENS ARE ROASTED TO 400° SO THAT THEY BROWN WELL IN THE SHORT COOKING TIME. THEY MAY ALSO BE DONE AT 325 BUT WILL TAKE LONGER AND WILL NOT BE AS BROWN. INCREASE COOKING TIME 15 TO 20 MINUTES FOR STUFFED CHICKEN AND DUCK.

◌ৎ Chicken Sausage Jambalaya ◌ৎ

2 TBSP	Peanut Oil		3 TBSP	Whole Basil
2 TBSP	Flour		¼ CUP	Cajun Seasoning, page 128
10½ CUPS	Chicken Stock		1 CUP	Tasso, ground
¼ LB	Butter		3 CUPS	Tomato, crushed
6 CUPS	Onion		½ CUP	Tomato Paste
3 CUPS	Bell Pepper		6-8 CUPS	Chicken, boneless, cubed
1½ CUPS	Celery		5 CUPS	Smoked Pork Sausage
3 TBSP	Garlic		5 CUPS	Rice, long grain or converted
¼ CUP	Parsley		1 CUP	Green Onion, chopped

(Continues)

In a 4-quart saucepan, heat oil and add flour. Whisk until dark brown. Add chicken stock and whisk until totally blended. Keep fire on high heat until a rolling boil for 15-20 minutes.

Meanwhile, chop and mince vegetables as desired. In a 12 quart pot, heat butter on high heat until totally melted and bubbly. Add onion, bell pepper, celery, garlic, parsley, basil, Cajun seasoning and stir well. Sauté on high until onions begin to wilt. Add tasso and stir well. Sauté another 5 minutes. Add crushed tomato and stir well. Bring back to bubble and add tomato paste; stir until totally blended. Add chicken stock mixture and stir well. Bring to rolling boil. Taste the mixture to test for seasoning. Mixture should be slightly too salty. Add pork sausage and stir well. Cook on high heat for 10 minutes, stirring occasionally.

Next add cooked chicken and stir in well. Bring back to boil and add uncooked rice and stir well. Bring back to rolling boil, stir well, cover and simmer on low heat for 10 minutes. Stir and cover for 5 minutes. Repeat until rice is 95% cooked. Cover, remove from heat, and let stand for at least 10 minutes. Add chopped green onion and stir well. Serve.

❧ Chicken Sauce Piquant ❧

2	Chicken Fryers (8 pieces each)	3 cups	Onions
1 cup	Vegetable Oil	3 tbsp	Garlic
½ cup	Bell Pepper	¼ cup	Fresh Parsley
1½ cups	Celery	2 quarts	Water
¼ cup	Green Onion	2 tsp	Salt
2	Bay Leaves	½ tsp	Black Pepper
2 cups	Mushrooms	2 tsp	Cayenne Pepper
¼ cup	Jalapeno Peppers	¾ cup	Rhine Wine
1 small can	Tomato Paste	10 dashes	Pepper Sauce
1 cup	Flour		

Chop all vegetables to a fine texture. Mince garlic and process jalapeno peppers in a food processor until very fine.

Salt chicken and brown in ¼ cup of vegetable oil. Add bell pepper, celery, green onion, bay leaf, mushrooms, jalapeno peppers and simmer for 15 minutes. Add tomato paste and cook 5 minutes more. Remove from heat and reserve.

In a separate large pot, heat ¾ cup oil and add flour. Stir over medium heat until dark brown (about 20-25 minutes). Add onions, garlic and parsley and stir. Add water slowly and stir until completely blended. Add salt, pepper, cayenne and stir. Cover and simmer on medium heat for 1 hour, stirring every 10 minutes. Add chicken mixture and stir well until mixture thickens. Add pepper sauce and wine, stir, cooking 20 minutes more on medium heat. Serve over spaghetti or rice. Top with parmesan cheese, if desired

❧ Apple Pepper Chicken ❧

6	Chicken Breasts, boneless	½ cup	Brown Sugar, firmly packed
2 cups	Apple Juice	1 tsp	Ground Cinnamon
2 tbsp	Butter	¼ tsp	Nutmeg
2 large	Apples	1 tbsp	Corn Starch
1 tbsp	Black Pepper	¼ cup	Water

Wash chicken, then pat dry. Soak chicken in apple juice for 2 hours in refrigerator. Remove chicken, reserve juice. In a 10" skillet, melt butter on high heat. Add chicken, reduce heat to medium. Peel and core apples, slice thin. Turn chicken once after browned, then add apple slices, cover and continue to simmer chicken until other side is browned. Add apple juice, pepper, brown sugar, cinnamon and nutmeg. Stir well and cover. Simmer 25 minutes. Mix cornstarch in water, add to bubbling mixture. Stir until thick. Serve.

❧ Blackened Duck ❧

6	Duck breasts, boned	½ tsp	Salt
1 tbsp	Cayenne	1 tsp	Black Pepper
2 tbsp	Oregano	1 tbsp	Paprika
1 tbsp	Ground Thyme	9 tbsp	Butter

In a bowl, blend cayenne, oregano, thyme, salt, black pepper and paprika. Wash duck, and dip into seasoning, moderately coating both sides. In a cast iron skillet, melt 2 tbsp butter and heat on high until it begins to smoke slightly. Lay 2 pieces of the coated duck in skillet. (Note: It will pop and smoke). Turn over and over every 30 seconds until outer coating is blackened. Pour butter from skillet into a bowl and scrape excess in bowl as well. Repeat the process until breasts are cooked. Use drippings to pour over duck and serve.

✒ CHICKEN ETOUFFEE' ✒

1 LARGE	CHICKEN FRYER	3 TBSP	GARLIC
2 QUARTS	WATER	3 TBSP	PARSLEY
½ CUP	VEGETABLE. OIL	1 TBSP	SALT
1½ CUPS	FLOUR	1 TBSP	BLACK PEPPER
¼ LB	BUTTER	2 TBSP	WHOLE BASIL
2 CUPS	ONION	½ TSP	CAYENNE PEPPER
1 CUP	BELL PEPPER	6 DASHES	PEPPER SAUCE
½ CUP	CELERY		

In a 4-quart pot, heat water to boiling. Add whole chicken to pot and boil until completely cooked (about 45 minutes). Remove chicken and allow to cool. While chicken is cooling, strain chicken stock, skim oil and return to high heat. Boil until reduced to about

1-quart stock, then remove from heat. Pick cooled chicken and reserve. Chop all vegetables fine.

In a skillet heat vegetable oil to hot and add ¾ cup flour. Whisk until dark brown (be careful not to burn). Remove and reserve roux.

In a 2-quart saucepan, heat butter on high heat. Add onions, bell peppers, celery, garlic and sauté until onions just begin to wilt. Add remaining flour and stir in well. Continue to stir until flour is the color of a paper bag. Slowly add 1-quart reduced chicken stock, whisking until completely blended. Bring to boil and add reserved dark brown roux and stir in well until blended. Bring to boil, add remaining ingredients except picked chicken, reduce heat to just maintain boil, cover and simmer for 30 minutes.

Add picked chicken and stir. Cover and simmer 5 minutes. Remove from heat and let stand covered for 10 minutes. Serve over rice or your favorite pasta. Serves 4-6.

❧ Stuffed Baked Chicken ❧

1	CHICKEN FRYER, LARGE (SAVE LIVERS, MINCE)
¼ LB	BUTTER
1 CUP	ONION, CHOPPED
2 TBSP	GARLIC, MINCED
3 TBSP	PARSLEY FLAKES
½ CUP	BELL PEPPER, CHOPPED
1 TBSP	CAJUN SEASONING, (PAGE 128)
½ LB	PORK, GROUND
½ LB	TURKEY, GROUND
3 CUPS	CHICKEN STOCK OR WATER
1 CUP	COOKED RICE
1 CUP	SEASONED BREAD CRUMBS

Variation: 12 large oysters, cleaned and blended in strained liquid can be substituted for chicken livers.

Clean chicken inside and out. Chop livers into a very fine texture. Trim excess skin from chicken. In a skillet heat butter on medium high heat. Add onion, garlic, parsley, bell pepper and Cajun seasoning. Sauté for 10 minutes, then add ground pork. Stir. Add ground turkey and stir until brown. Add minced livers or oysters and stir into simmering mixture.

Add 1 cup of stock or water and bring to a bubble. Remove from heat. Add rice and stir in. Slowly add bread crumbs until texture holds together. Let cool. Then stuff chicken cavity. Put any remaining stuffing in a casserole dish to serve with dinner.

Preheat oven to 350°F. Place stuffed chicken in a baking pan. Pour 2 cups stock or water into pan, cover with foil and place in center of oven. Cook for 45 minutes. Remove foil. Raise heat to 400°F and bake another 15 to 20 minutes, or until brown. Serve.

NOTES

❧ If You Fry It, They Will Come ❧

Fried Catfish Fillets 77
Fried Okra 78
Stuffed Fried Shrimp..80
Tempura Batter for Fried Vegetables 83
Fried Mushrooms 84
Cajun Fried Chicken 86
Onion Rings...87
Fried Turkey 88
Fried Corn on the Cob...92
Fried Crawfish 93
Pan Fried Pork Chops..94
Pannéd Round 95
Corn Puppies..96
Shrimp Boulettes..98
Fried Soft Shell Crabs..99

❧ Total Volume of Various Special Baking Pans ❧

Tube Pans:	7½x3-inch "Bundt" tube pan	6 cups
	9x3½-inch fancy tube or "Bundt" pan	9 cups
	9x3½-inch angel cake pan	12 cups
	10x3¾-inch "Bundt" or "Crownburst" pan	12 cups
	9x3½-inch fancy tube mold	12 cups
	10x4-inch fancy tube mold (Kugelhupf)	16 cups
	10x4-inch angel cake pan	18 cups
Melon Mold:	7x5½x4-inch mold	6 cups
Spring-Form Pans:	8x3-inch pan	12 cups
	9x3-inch pan	16 cups
Ring Molds:	8½x2¼-inch mold	4½ cups
	9¼x2¾-inch mold	8 cups
Charlotte Mold:	6x4¼-inch mold	7½ cups
Brioche Pan:	9½x3¼-inch pan	8 cups

ଏ If You Fry It, They Will Come ଭ

I was standing in a vast okra field in south Louisiana. The wind was moving gently from the south. The sun was behind one of the only clouds in the sky, and the air was moist and cool for this time of year. As I walked through the head-high okra, feeling the leaves and inspecting the tubular vegetable, I thought I heard a voice…nah, must be my imagination, or maybe someone across the field was talking and the wind was carrying their voices. Yeah, that must be it. I continued to enjoy the breeze and the plentiful bounty when I heard it again; this time I understood the voice. "If you fry it, they will come…if you fry it, they will come." It freaked me out at first, and I ran to the car and got out of there. The words kept going through my mind; if you fry it, they will come. I eventually realized that the voice must want me to have a party. That must be it; have a party with all your friends and neighbors for a fish fry.

75

(CONTINUES)

I immediately began to invite everyone over for the very next weekend. I was sure this was what the voice wanted, because everyone could make it. The party was a great success. I saw people I didn't even know. One of them came to me: "Is this heaven?, he asked. "No," I told him, "this is Louisiana."

Just as everything began to wind down and everyone had gone, I was cleaning the yard when I heard the voice again. "Ease their hunger pain," it said. Could the voice be saying that the party was not enough? Could it be that the voice wanted me to share these great Cajun recipes with as many people as possible? Well, when the voice came to me in a dream and said, "Go the distance," then I knew what I had to do. Since this book's completion there are no more voices (except for when my wife yells, "Are you going to clean up this kitchen?").

❦ Fried Catfish Fillets ❧

2 LB	Catfish Fillets
1 LB	Corn Flour or Corn Meal
1 TBSP	Cajun Seasoning, (page 128)
½ CUP	Prepared Yellow Mustard
2 CUPS	Oil for Frying

Clean catfish with cool water, rubbing your hands over the entire surface, feeling for any bones that might be left. Cut any bones away. After rinsing clean, pat dry with a towel. Place fish in a bowl with mustard. With your hands mix mustard and catfish until evenly coated. In a separate bowl, mix corn flour (or meal) and Cajun seasoning with a wire whisk. Dip catfish in dry mixture until coated. In a 10 inch skillet, heat oil to hot. Fry fillets, turning over every 3 minutes until brown. Serves 4.

❧ Fried Okra ❧

1 LB	OKRA, FRESH OR FROZEN
1	EGG
1 CUP	MILK
1 TSP	SALT
1 TSP	CAYENNE PEPPER
1 TSP	WHITE PEPPER
1 TBSP	DIJON MUSTARD
2 CUPS	ALL PURPOSE FLOUR
1 QUART	OIL FOR FRYING

In a 1½-quart or larger bowl, beat egg. Add milk, salt, cayenne pepper, white pepper and dijon mustard. Blend or whip together until completely mixed. Slowly add flour as you continue to blend. (Note: you can do this in a food processor with the blade attachment if you like.) Set aside. Prepare the okra. If your okra is not sliced, wash okra well (if your okra is sliced, chances are that it has already been washed by the packer). Cut off the tip of the okra just about ¾ inch from the end. Remove the hard stem top of the okra. Slice the okra in ½ inch slices.

Preheat oil to 400°F. When oil is hot, dip okra in batter, a few at a time. With a fork, remove okra from batter and drop into hot oil. Fry until golden brown, remove from oil and drain. Serves 3-4.

ഔ STUFFED FRIED SHRIMP ඏ

1 LB	JUMBO SHRIMP (16-20 PER LB.)	2 TBSP	PARSLEY, MINCED
¼ LB	SMALL SHRIMP (70-90 PER LB.)	2 TBSP	WHOLE BASIL
2 TBSP	BUTTER	2 TSP	SALT
½ CUP	ONION, MINCED	2 TSP	BLACK PEPPER
¼ CUP	BELL PEPPER, MINCED	1 TSP	WHOLE THYME
2 TBSP	CELERY, MINCED	4 CUPS	SEASONED BREAD CRUMBS
2 TBSP	GARLIC, MINCED	1 QUART	OIL FOR FRYING

First peel shrimp and remove heads. Leave the tails on the jumbo shrimp only. Place all peeling and heads in a 1 quart pot with 3 cups water and boil for 40 minutes. Strain liquid from pot, discard peeling and heads, then return liquid to cleaned pot. Boil until reduced by half. Reserve stock.

Next, in a 10 inch skillet, melt butter on high heat. Add onion, bell pepper, celery, garlic, parsley flakes and basil. Simmer on high heat until onion begin to clear. Add salt, pepper, thyme and mix well. Cover and simmer on low heat for 5 minutes. Chop small shrimp to medium fine texture and add to skillet, along with ¾ cup reserved shrimp stock, and stir well. Bring heat back to high and simmer until mixture begins to boil. Cover and simmer on low heat for 15 minutes, stirring frequently.

While mixture is simmering, clean, butterfly and devein jumbo shrimp by slicing down the back of the shrimp, cutting about ¾ of the way through the shrimp. Remove the dark vein and rinse well. Reserve, covered, until ready to stuff.

Remove skillet from heat after 15 minutes of simmering and stir well. Add bread crumbs to mixture, and stir well until mixture becomes firm enough to handle. It should take between 1½ to 1¾ cups of bread crumbs. Allow mixture to cool. Reserve remaining bread crumbs.

(CONTINUES)

When mixture has cooled, spoon a generous amount (about 2 oz.) of stuffing onto the butterflied shrimp. Mold stuffing around the end of the shrimp with your hands, then roll stuffed shrimp in remaining bread crumbs. In a 2 quart pot heat oil to 400°F. Carefully drop stuffed shrimp in oil and fry until brown. Remove, drain and serve. Serves 4-5.

∽ TEMPURA BATTER FOR FRIED VEGETABLES ∾

2	EGGS	1 CUP	MILK
2 TSP	SALT	2 CUPS	SELF RISING FLOUR

Mix all ingredients in a bowl. Cut about 3 cups assorted vegetables into bite sized pieces. For example: broccoli florets, cauliflower florets, carrot sticks, bell pepper, onion, zucchini, green onion, eggplant, etc.

Dip vegetables in batter and fry in hot oil (350°F) until brown. Serve with favorite sauce, dip or just as is. Serves 4-5 as an appetizer.

✆ Fried Mushrooms ✆

1 LB	Fresh Mushrooms, small to medium size
1	Egg
¾ cup	Milk
1 cup	All Purpose Flour
3½ cups	Corn Flour (Fish Fry)
1 tbsp + 1 tsp	Cajun Seasoning, (page 128)
1 tbsp	Salt
2 tbsp	Parsley Flakes
1 quart	Oil for Frying

Clean mushrooms and trim bottom of stem. In a large bowl, whip egg and milk. Add flour and ½ cup corn flour. Blend well. Add 1 tsp Cajun seasoning, ½ tbsp salt and parsley flakes and blend well. In a separate bowl combine 3 cups corn flour with 1 tbsp Cajun seasoning and ½ tbsp salt.

In a 2-quart pot heat oil to 400°F. Put mushrooms in egg mixture and str until all mushrooms are equally coated. Place mushrooms, one at a time, in corn flour mixture and roll around until completely coated. Shake off excess. When all are done, carefully drop into hot oil and fry until brown. Serve with ketchup, cocktail sauce, creamy ranch dressing or your favorite sauce.

✺ CAJUN FRIED CHICKEN ✺

1	CHICKEN FRYER, CUT INTO 8 PIECES	1 CUP	FLOUR
2	EGGS	2 CUPS	CORN FLOUR
1 CUP	RANCH STYLE SALAD DRESSING	1 TBSP	SALT
1 CUP	CAJUN SEASONING, (PAGE 128)	1 QUART	OIL FOR FRYING
1 TSP	SALT		

Wash chicken well. Pat dry with a towel. Place in large bowl. In a separate bowl combine eggs, ranch dressing, Cajun seasoning and 1 tsp salt. Whip with a wire whisk until well mixed and creamy. In a separate bowl mix flour, corn flour and 1 tbsp salt. Dredge chicken pieces in dry mixture, then dip into the egg mixture, then back into the dry mixture and roll until completely coated. If you like, you can repeat the process for extra thick coating. Heat oil to 300°F. Fry until golden brown. Serves 4.

✆ Onion Rings ✆

2 LARGE	ONIONS	8 CUPS	FLOUR
2 LARGE	EGGS		SALT TO TASTE
2 CUPS	MILK	1½ QUARTS	OIL FOR FRYING

Cut off ends of onions and peel outer skin. Slice onions ¼ to ½ inch thick. Press out all rings and reserve. In a large bowl, mix eggs and milk, then whip until totally blended. Slowly add 2 cups flour, a little at a time, while whipping until all is added and totally blended. In another large bowl, place remaining flour. In a 2-quart pot, heat oil to 400°F. Dip onions in egg mixture until completely coated. Next, dredge coated onion rings into flour until completely coated. Carefully drop coated rings in hot oil and fry until lightly browned. Drain on paper towels, sprinkle salt to taste and serve. Serves 2.

✑ FRIED TURKEY ✑

½ LB	BUTTER
1 TSP	PEPPER SAUCE
1 TBSP	CAJUN SEASONING, (PAGE 128)
¼ CUP	ONION JUICE
¼ CUP	GARLIC JUICE
¼ CUP	WHITE WINE WORCESTERSHIRE SAUCE
1	SYRINGE TYPE MEAT INJECTOR
1 13-15 LB	TURKEY
5 GALLONS	PEANUT OIL
40 QUART	POT FOR FRYING

This procedure requires an outdoor portable fryer, i.e., single jet or low pressure burner

This procedure requires an outdoor portable fryer, i.e., single jet or low pressure burner capable of high heat and low heat adjustability. The large size pot is necessary because the hot oil will boil when the cold turkey is added.

WARNING! This is a very dangerous process and requires a great deal of responsibility. Follow instructions carefully. Keep children, and, for that matter, everyone away from the pot of oil, especially when placing the turkey into the hot oil and when taking the turkey out. Be sure to have one person there to assist you to remove the turkey from the oil when done.

If turkey is frozen, you must thaw completely. Refrigerate turkey until you are ready to inject. In a 1-quart saucepan, heat butter on high heat. Add pepper sauce, Cajun seasoning, onion juice, garlic juice and white wine Worcestershire, and bring to boil. Simmer uncovered on medium high heat for 15 minutes, stirring occasionally. Remove from heat and allow to cool.

(CONTINUES)

When injection mixture is cooled to room temperature, remove turkey from refrigerator and inject the butter mixture into turkey with syringe type meat injector. Choose several meaty locations of the turkey to inject the mixture. You may need to hold the injection spot with your finger until the butter mixture solidifies enough to stop leaking. Continue the process until all of the butter mixture is injected into the turkey. Next, tie the legs of the turkey together with several layers of heat-resistant string (enough to support the weight of the turkey). Test this before proceeding. Next, tie a long loop of string or wire around the inside of the tied legs. Make this loop long enough to hang outside of the pot when the turkey is frying. This will be used to safely place the turkey into and remove from the hot oil. Put the turkey back into the refrigerator until ready to fry.

Heat oil on a high heat capacity burner until oil is 325°F. CAREFULLY place the turkey into the hot oil until totally submerged. Allow turkey to fry for 45 minutes. To check if the turkey is done, carefully remove turkey. (Oil will be in the cavity of the turkey. Allow all oil to drip out before completely removing). With a meat thermometer, check the breast at the thickest part of the bird. Temperature should be between 160°F and 170°F. Slice just like you would at Thanksgiving. Serves 8 - 10.

Note: For best results, be sure to maintain recommended frying temperature.

❧ Fried Corn on the Cob ❧

½ CUP	CREOLE MUSTARD
4 CUPS	CORN FLOUR OR CORN MEAL
1 TBSP	CAJUN SEASONING, (PAGE 128)
6	MINI EARS OF CORN, FRESH OR FROZEN
1 QUART	OIL FOR FRYING

Heat oil to 400°F. Roll corn in creole mustard until coated. In a separate bowl mix corn flour (or corn meal) with Cajun seasoning until blended. Roll coated corn in flour, pressing down until completely coated around the kernels and on the sides. Fry in hot oil until coating is golden brown. Serves 6 (if it gets to the table).

⚙ Fried Crawfish ⚙

1	Egg
1 CUP	Milk
1 TSP	Salt
1 TSP	Cajun Seasoning, (page 128)
4 CUPS	Corn Flour
1 QUART	Oil for Frying
1 LB	Crawfish, peeled

In a bowl, mix egg, milk, salt and Cajun seasoning. Whip with a fork or whisk until totally blended. Add 1 cup corn flour and whip until blended. Heat oil to 400°F. Drop crawfish into egg mixture, and mix until coated. In a separate bowl place remaining corn flour. Roll coated crawfish tails into the corn flour mixture until coated. Carefully drop crawfish tails into oil and fry until golden brown. Serves 4.

❧ PAN FRIED PORK CHOPS ❧

6	PORK CHOPS, THINLY CUT
1	LARGE ONION, CUT IN RINGS
1 TSP	SALT
1 TSP	BLACK PEPPER
2 TBSP	BUTTER
½ TBSP	FLOUR
½ CUP	WATER

Heat skillet (preferably cast iron) on high heat. Place moderately trimmed pork chops in pan and fry on each side for 3 minutes. Place onion rings over chops and cover pan. Reduce heat and simmer 5 minutes each side. Remove chops and onions from skillet. Return to high heat. Add butter and melt. Add flour and whisk into butter. Add water and stir. Add chops and onions back to skillet, cover and simmer another 15 minutes on low. Serves 3.

❧ Pannéd Round ❧

2 LARGE	EGGS	2 LB	BEEF OR VEAL ROUND, THINLY CUT
1 TSP	SALT	4 CUPS	SEASONED BREAD CRUMBS
1 TSP	BLACK PEPPER		OIL FOR FRYING

In a bowl beat eggs with salt and black pepper. Next, cut round in 4 inch long strips as wide as the natural separation of the meat will allow, but no wider than 2 to 3", cutting away all fat. Sprinkle bread crumbs in a plate. Dredge sliced round in egg mixture and lay on top of bread crumbs. Sprinkle bread crumbs on top and pat in. Turn to make sure meat is coated. In a 10" skillet, heat ½ inch of vegetable oil on high heat for 4 minutes. Carefully lay breaded round in oil and fry, browning on both sides, until a deep golden brown. Serves 6 with side dish.

∽ CORN PUPPIES ∾

1½ CUPS	ALL PURPOSE FLOUR
2 CUPS	CORN FLOUR OR CORN MEAL
¼ TSP	BAKING POWDER
¼ CUP	SUGAR
¼ LB	BUTTER, melted
¾ CUP	MILK
2 LARGE	EGGS
1 15OZ CAN	WHOLE KERNEL CORN, DRAINED
4 CUPS	OIL for FRYING
¼ TO ½ CUP	POWDERED SUGAR

In a mixing bowl combine all purpose flour, corn flour (or corn meal) baking powder and sugar. Blend with a mixer on medium high speed until totally blended. Continue to mix while adding butter a little at a time. Continue to blend until pea-sized balls are formed. Slowly add milk to mixture while mixing on high speed. Add eggs and blend until creamy thick texture (note: mixture should be firm). Add drained corn to mixture and fold until evenly mixed.

Next, in a 1½-quart pot, heat oil to 300°F. Carefully spoon 2 to 3 tbsp of mixture into hot oil. As puppies begin to brown, turn over a couple of times until evenly browned all over. Remove and drain on paper towels. To serve, place in a bowl and sprinkle powdered sugar on top with a wire strainer. Serves 6-8.

✐ Shrimp Boulettes ✐

¼ CUP	CELERY		1 CUP	FLOUR
1 CUP	ONIONS, CHOPPED		1 CUP	SEASONED BREAD CRUMBS
¼ CUP	GREEN ONIONS		1 TSP	SALT
1 CUP	SHRIMP		1 TSP	PEPPER
2	EGGS, BEATEN		2 CUPS	OIL FOR FRYING

Grind celery, onions and green onions in a food processor. Drain excess liquid, then empty mixture into a mixing bowl. Grind raw, peeled, minced shrimp in a food processor. Add to mixture and blend. Add eggs and blend completely.

Add flour and bread crumbs to mixture until you achieve a thick, pasty consistency. Add salt, pepper and mix. In a 2-quart pot, heat oil to hot. Spoon tablespoon-sized balls into hot oil and cook until browned. Serve.

✑ FRIED SOFT SHELL CRABS ✑

½ CUP	PREPARED YELLOW MUSTARD
⅓ TBSP	CAJUN SEASONING, (PAGE 128)
1 TSP	SALT
6	SOFT SHELL CRABS, CLEANED (SMALL TO MEDIUM)
4 CUPS	CORN FLOUR (OR FISH FRY)
4 CUPS	OIL FOR FRYING

In a bowl mix mustard, Cajun seasoning and salt until well blended. Roll soft shell crabs in mustard mixture until moderately coated. In a 1½-quart pot, heat oil on high heat until 350°F. Roll the crabs in corn flour mixture until completely coated. Fry on each side 3 to 4 minutes or until nicely browned. Drain on paper towels. Serves 3.

∽ NOTES ∾

∽ IDANO ∾

CAJUN CORNBREAD DRESSING 102

CAJUN SMOTHERED POTATOES 104

STUFFED BELL PEPPERS #1
   SHRIMP AND GROUND TURKEY 106

STUFFED BELL PEPPERS #2
   CRABMEAT AND SHRIMP 108

STUFFED PEPPER PASTA 110

ALLIGATOR SAUCE PIQUANT 112

RED BEANS AND RICE 114

❧ Substitutions for a Missing Ingredient ❧

1 Square Chocolate, 1 ounce	3 or 4 tbsp cocoa plus ½ tbsp fat
1 tbsp Cornstarch, for thickening	2 tbsp flour
1 cup All Purpose Flour, sifted	1 cup plus 2 tbsp sifted cake flour
1 cup Cake Flour, sifted	1 cup minus 2 tbsp sifted all purpose flour
1 tsp Baking Powder	¼ tsp baking soda plus ½ tsp cream of tartar
1 cup Sour Milk	1 cup buttermilk, let stand for 5 minutes or 1 cup sweet milk into which 1 tbsp vinegar or lemon juice has been stirred
1 cup Sweet Milk	1 cup sour milk or buttermilk plus ½ tsp baking soda
¾ cup Cracker Crumbs	1 cup bread crumbs
1 cup Cream, sour, heavy	⅓ cup butter and ⅔ cup milk in any sour milk recipe
1 tsp Dried Herbs	1 tbsp fresh herbs
1 cup Whole Milk	½ cup evaporated milk and ½ cup water or 1 cup reconstituted nonfat dry milk and 1 tbsp butter
1 package Active Dry Yeast	1 cake compressed yeast
1 tbsp Instant Minced Onion, rehydrated	1 small fresh onion
1 tbsp Prepared Mustard	1 tsp dry mustard
⅛ tsp Garlic Powder	1 small pressed clove of garlic
1 lb Whole Dates	1½ cup pitted and cut dates
3 medium Bananas	1 cup mashed bananas
3 cups dry Corn Flakes	1 cup crushed corn flakes
10 miniature Marshmallows	1 large marshmallow

༒ "IDANO" ༒

This section is called "IDANO" because the nature of the recipes is difficult to categorize. The ingredients will have a main ingredient but will have other significant ingredients that greatly influence the finished product. The presence of these ingredients make it difficult to determine what to call the recipe. When this happens "I DON'T KNOW" how to place this recipe in a particular section. I'm sure you will enjoy the recipes in this section. I do know that Cajun cooking is often the culmination of several primary ingredients to achieve the best tasting food Cajuns have been enjoying for years. Try 'em, you'll like 'em.

⟋⟍ Cajun Cornbread Dressing ⟍⟋

4 8½-oz	Packages Corn Muffin Mix	1 lb	Ground Beef
½ lb	Butter	2 cups	Chicken Stock
1 cup	Onion, chopped	1¼ cup	Cream of Mushroom Soup
½ cup	Bell Pepper, chopped	1 tbsp	Salt
¼ cup	Celery, chopped	2 tbsp	Cajun Seasoning, (page 128)
2 tbsp	Garlic, minced	6	Eggs
2 tbsp	Parsley, dried	3 cups	Milk
1 lb	Ground Pork	1 cup	Green Onion

First prepare cornbread as per package instructions, using ½ lb. melted butter to grease the pan. Bake as instructed, and allow to cool. Next, in a 4-quart pot, heat remaining butter on high heat. Add onion, bell pepper, celery, garlic and parsley. Sauté for 5 minutes. Add ground pork and sauté until pork begins to brown. Break up the pork as much as possible. Add the ground beef and stir well, breaking up as much as possible. Continue to brown meat until totally cooked. Remove from heat and drain out excess oil. Add chicken stock and return to high heat. Bring to boil and boil for 10 minutes. Add cream of mushroom soup and stir until blended. Add salt and Cajun seasoning and stir well. Reduce heat to low and simmer for 20 minutes. Remove from heat. In a large mixing bowl, crumble cornbread well. Preheat oven to 350°F. Slowly mix crumbled cornbread and meat mixture until blended. Add milk to mixture and mix well. Next, add beaten eggs and green onion and mix until totally blended. Grease a 9" x 13" pan. Spread cornbread mixture evenly in pan and bake at 350°F for 25-30 minutes, or until center is firm. Serves 8-10.

❧ Cajun Smothered Potatoes ❧

8 LB	Russet Potatoes	¼ CUP	Whole Basil
½ LB	Butter	2 TBSP	Paprika
¼ CUP	Bacon Fat	2 TBSP	Cajun Seasoning, (page 128)
2 CUPS	Onion, chopped	2 TBSP	Salt
1 CUP	Bell Pepper, chopped	2 CUPS	Ground Tasso
½ CUP	Celery, chopped	1 CUP	Chicken Stock
¼ CUP	Garlic, minced	2 CUPS	Green Onion
¼ CUP	Parsley, dried		

Peel potatoes and cut into medium sized cubes. Rinse well, cover with water, bring to boil for 16 minutes. Preheat oven to 400°F. In a oven roaster on top the stove melt butter on high heat. As soon as butter is melted, add bacon fat, onion, bell pepper, celery, garlic, parsley, whole basil, paprika, Cajun seasoning and salt. Stir well and sauté for 10 minutes. Add ground tasso and stir well. Put roaster (uncovered) in oven and begin to bake at preheated temperature. After 10 minutes in the oven, add chicken stock and stir well. Bake another 20 minutes, stirring every 10 minutes.

Drain potatoes completely and let stand uncovered. Potatoes should be about 75% cooked.

Add partially cooked potatoes to oven roaster. Stir well. Continue to bake (stirring occasionally) for another 20 minutes. Remove from oven and cover roaster. Let stand for 10 minutes. Add green onions and stir well. Serves 20 normal servings.

❧ STUFFED BELL PEPPERS #1 ❧
SHRIMP AND GROUND TURKEY

1½ QUARTS	WATER	3 TSP	SALT
1 TBSP	VEGETABLE OIL	1 CUP	MUSHROOMS, MINCED
¾ CUP	RICE, UNCOOKED	1 LB	GROUND TURKEY
2	SMALL BELL PEPPERS, MINCED	1 TSP	BLACK PEPPER
1	LARGE ONION, MINCED	¼ CUP	SEASONED BREAD CRUMBS,
3 TBSP	PARSLEY FLAKES		OPTIONAL
4	LARGE BELL PEPPERS, WHOLE	1 LB	SHRIMP
1 TBSP	GARLIC, MINCED	3 QUARTS	WATER

In a 2 quart pot heat water to a boil. Add 1 tsp salt to boiling water. Add rice to water and stir to keep rice separate. Cover and reduce heat to simmer. Set timer for 15 minutes. When timer goes, off immediately cool with cold tap water, pour rice in a colander and continue to cool with cold tap water until rice stays separate. This is to stop the rice from cooking. Meanwhile:

In a large skillet heat oil on high heat. Stir in onion, minced bell pepper, garlic, parsley, mushrooms, 1 tsp salt and pepper. Sauté until onions are clear. Add ground turkey, stirring and breaking up until browned. Add shrimp and stir 5 more minutes, remove from heat. Add rice and stir in until mixed well.

In a 4-quart pot boil 3 quarts water with remaining salt. Cut whole bell peppers in half stem to stern. Cut out stem and seed, leaving as much pepper as possible. Parboil peppers for 2-3 minutes, remove and drain. Preheat oven to 350°F. Lay peppers in a baking pan and stuff with mixture. Top with bread crumbs (optional). Bake for 20 minutes covered and 10 minutes uncovered, or until brown. Serves 8.

⮞ STUFFED BELL PEPPER #2 ⮜
CRABMEAT AND SHRIMP

3 TBSP	VEGETABLE OIL	1 TBSP	CAJUN SEASONING, (PAGE 128)
1	SMALL BELL PEPPER, MINCED	¼ TSP	THYME
1	LARGE ONION, MINCED	2 CUPS	PEELED TOMATOES, DRAINED
1 CUP	CELERY, MINCED	1 LB	SHRIMP, PEELED AND DEVEINED
3 TBSP	GARLIC, MINCED	8 OZ	VELVEETA CHEESE
2 TBSP	PARSLEY FLAKES	1 LB	CRABMEAT, CLEANED OF ALL SHELL
1 TSP	BLACK PEPPER	4	LARGE BELL PEPPERS, WHOLE

In a 10" skillet heat oil on high heat. Add minced bell pepper, onion, celery, garlic, parsley, pepper, Cajun seasoning and thyme. Sauté until onions are clear and very tender. Add drained tomatoes and stir until tomatoes liquefy. Add shrimp and stir 5 minutes, then reduce heat. Add Velveeta cheese and stir until melted. Add crabmeat and mix in well. Remove from heat.

Prepare and stuff large peppers as described in # 1 (page 107). Preheat oven to 350°F and bake 20 minutes covered and 10 minutes uncovered, or until lightly browned on top. Serves 8.

∽ Stuffed Pepper Pasta ∾

4 TBSP	BUTTER		1 TSP	SALT
2 CUPS	ONION, CHOPPED		1 TSP	BLACK PEPPER
2 CUPS	BELL PEPPER, CHOPPED		½ TSP	CAYENNE PEPPER
½ CUP	CELERY, CHOPPED		3 DASHES	PEPPER SAUCE
1 TBSP	GARLIC, MINCED		1 CUP	GREEN ONION, CHOPPED
3 TBSP	PARSLEY FLAKES		8 OZ	MOZZARELLA, GRATED
1 LB	LEAN GROUND BEEF (80%)		8 OZ	CHEDDAR CHEESE, GRATED
½ LB	COOKED SHRIMP		½ CUP	PARMESAN, GRATED
1¼ CUP	CREAM OF MUSHROOM SOUP		4 CUPS	COOKED ASSORTED PASTA
1 CUP	CHICKEN STOCK OR WATER			YOUR CHOICE
1 TSP	WHOLE BASIL			

In a 6-quart pot, heat butter until melted. Add onion, green pepper, celery, garlic, parsley and stir well. Sauté for 5 minutes on high heat. Add ground beef and stir, breaking the meat up as it cooks. Add shrimp and stir well. Add cream of mushroom soup and stir well. Add chicken stock (or water) and stir well. Bring to a rapid bubble, stir, then add mozzarella and cheddar cheeses. Remove from heat. Stir in cheese well. Add pasta and stir until well mixed. Top with chopped fresh green onion and parmesan cheese and serve.

∽ Alligator Sauce Piquant ∾

¾ CUP	VEGETABLE OIL	½ LB	FRESH MUSHROOMS, SLICED
1 CUP	ALL PURPOSE FLOUR	1 CUP	JALAPENO PEPPER, FINELY MINCED
2 CUPS	ONION, CHOPPED	½ CUP	WHITE WINE
1 CUP	BELL PEPPER, CHOPPED	2 LB	ALLIGATOR BODY MEAT, CUBED ½"
½ CUP	CELERY, CHOPPED	1 TBSP	SALT
¼ CUP	GARLIC, MINCED	1 TBSP	BLACK PEPPER
¼ CUP	PARSLEY FLAKES	1 TSP	CAYENNE PEPPER
2 CUPS	TOMATO, CRUSHED	1 TSP	WHOLE THYME
¼ CUP	TOMATO PASTE	2 TBSP	WHOLE SWEET BASIL
1¼ CUP	DICED ROTEL TOMATO		COOKED RICE OR PASTA
1 QUART	CHICKEN STOCK		

With oil and flour make a dark roux. Reduce heat to very low and add onion, bell pepper, celery, garlic and parsley (stirring as you add each). Add crushed tomato and stir well. Return to high heat. Add tomato paste and stir until blended. Add rotel tomato and continue to stir. Add chicken stock slowly, stirring to blend. Add jalapeno peppers and mushrooms and stir. Add wine. Bring to boil and reduce heat to maintain low boil. Simmer for 45 minutes to an hour. Add alligator meat and remaining ingredients (except for rice or pasta) and continue to simmer until alligator meat is cooked and tender. This should take about 30 minutes. Serve over cooked rice or pasta.

✎ Red Beans and Rice ✎

1 LB	RED KIDNEY BEANS		1 TBSP	PARSLEY FLAKES
3 QUARTS	WATER		2 TBSP	SALT
2 CUPS	ONIONS, CHOPPED		2 TBSP	BLACK PEPPER
1 CUP	BELL PEPPER, CHOPPED		2 TBSP	CHILI POWDER
½ CUP	CELERY, CHOPPED		2 LB	SMOKED PORK SAUSAGE
2 TBSP	GARLIC, MINCED			

Wash beans well, then drain. In a 6-quart pot, cover beans with 3" water (about 3 qts.). Allow beans to soak for several hours if possible. Chop vegetables to a fine consistency. After soaking, heat beans on high heat until boiling. Take out half of beans, reserve. Add onions, bell pepper, celery, garlic and parsley. Stir well. Bring to hard boil, reduce heat to maintain boil. Stir often and add water to maintain level as needed. Add salt, black pepper, chili powder, reserved beans and sausage and simmer boil for 2 hours. Serve over rice.

ᥱ SEAFOOD SECTION ᥲ

SHRIMP RICE 115
REDFISH COURTBOUILLION 116
CAJUN CRAB PIE 118
CRAWFISH FETTUCCINE 120
SHRIMP IN A CAJUN BUCKET..122
TROUT SUPREME 124
CRAB BOIL 126

∽ Contents of Cans ∾

Size:	Average Contents
8-oz.	1 cup
Picnic	1¼ cups
No. 300	1¾ cups
No. 1 tall	2 cups
No. 303	2 cups
No. 2	2½ cups
No. 2½	3½ cups
No. 3	4 cups
No. 10	12 to 13 cups

Of the different sizes of cans used by commercial canners, these are the most common.

∽ General Oven Chart ∾

Very slow oven	250° to 300°F
Slow Oven	300° to 325°F
Moderate Oven	325° to 375°F
Medium Hot Oven	375° to 400°F
Hot Oven	400° to 450°F
Very Hot Oven	450° to 500°F

❦ SHRIMP RICE ❦

1 TBSP	OIL	1 TBSP	GARLIC, MINCED
1 LB	SHRIMP, PEELED AND DEVEINED	¼ CUP	PARSLEY, MINCED
½ CUP	BUTTER	¼ CUP	MUSHROOMS, SLICED
½ CUP	GREEN ONION, CHOPPED	3 CUPS	COOKED RICE
1 CUP	ONION, CHOPPED	3 TBSP	GRATED PARMESAN CHEESE,
			OPTIONAL

In a skillet heat oil on high and cook shrimp for 10 minutes. Remove shrimp from skillet, drain completely and add butter. To melted butter, add green onion, onion, garlic, parsley, mushrooms; let simmer 10-12 minutes on medium heat. Stir occasionally. Add cooked rice and stir until evenly mixed. Add cooked shrimp and mix well. Serve as is or top with parmesan cheese.

❧ Redfish Courtbouillion ❧

1 CUP	FLOUR	1 CUP	CELERY, CHOPPED
¾ CUP	OIL	1 QUART	HOT WATER
1 CUP	ONIONS, CHOPPED MEDIUM	1 CUP	PARSLEY, MINCED
½ CUP	BELL PEPPER, CHOPPED	1 CUP	WHITE WINE
2 CUPS	STEWED TOMATOES	¼ CUP	OLIVES
2 SMALL CANS	TOMATO PASTE	1 CUP	FRESH MUSHROOMS, QUARTERED
2 TBSP	GARLIC, MINCED	4-5 LBS	REDFISH FILLETS
3	BAY LEAVES	1 TSP	SALT
1	LEMON, THINLY SLICED	1 TSP	BLACK PEPPER
1 CUP	CELERY, CHOPPED		

In a cast iron pot, make a medium brown roux with flour and oil. Do this by heating oil on a medium high heat until hot and add flour, stirring constantly until flour turns a dark brown (about the color of a chocolate bar). Add onions, bell pepper and sauté until brown. Add tomatoes (rotel if desired) and cook until liquid is gone. Add garlic, celery, lemon slices and bay leaves. Add water a little at a time. Cook for 15 to 20 minutes. After boiling begins, add parsley, wine, olives and mushrooms. Stir well, then add fish and stir in lightly. Add salt and pepper, reduce heat and cook 15 to 20 minutes until fish is cooked; do not stir.

Let stand covered for a few minutes. Serve over rice. Serves 10-12 people (or 3-4 Cajuns).

∾ Cajun Crab Pie ∾

1 CUP	ONION, CHOPPED	2 TSP	SALT
1½ CUPS	GREEN ONION, CHOPPED	1 TSP	CAYENNE PEPPER
¼ CUP	BELL PEPPER, CHOPPED	2 TSP	BLACK PEPPER
1 TBSP	GARLIC, MINCED	1 LB	CHEDDAR CHEESE, SHREDDED
3 TBSP	BUTTER	3 TBSP	LEMON JUICE
1 LB	LUMP CRABMEAT, PICKED CLEAN OF SHELL		

∾ The Crust: ∾

1 CUP	SELF-RISING FLOUR	¼ TSP	BAKING SODA
1 TBSP	DRY MILK	1 CUP	MILK
1 TSP	SUGAR	3	EGGS
1 TSP	SALT	1 TBSP	BUTTER

Preheat oven to 350°F. In a skillet, sauté onion, green onion, bell pepper and garlic in 3 tbsp butter until onion is clear. Remove from heat and add crabmeat, salt, cayenne and black pepper. In a separate bowl combine flour, dry milk, sugar, salt, baking soda, milk, eggs and 1 tbsp butter, blend until smooth. Pour into greased 9" x 12" baking pan. Top with prepared crab mixture. Cover with shredded cheese and sprinkle with lemon juice. Bake covered for 35 minutes at 350°F. Uncover and bake at 400°F until brown. Serves 6-8.

Crawfish Fettuccine

¼ LB	BUTTER	2 TSP	BLACK PEPPER
1 CUP	ONION, CHOPPED	1 TSP	CAYENNE PEPPER
½ CUP	BELL PEPPER, CHOPPED	1 LB	CRAWFISH, PEELED
¼ CUP	CELERY, CHOPPED	3 CUPS	HEAVY CREAM
2 TBSP	GARLIC, MINCED	1 LB	VELVEETA CHEESE
2 TBSP	PARSLEY FLAKES	1 CUP	GRATED PARMESAN CHEESE
2 TBSP	WHOLE BASIL	1 LB	FETTUCCINE, COOKED
2 TSP	SALT	1 CUP	GREEN ONION, CHOPPED

In a 3-quart saucepan, heat butter to hot. Add onion, bell pepper, celery, garlic, parsley, basil, and sauté on high until onions begin to wilt. Add salt, black pepper, cayenne pepper, crawfish and sauté for 10 minutes. Add heavy cream and stir well. Cover, reduce heat to low, and simmer for 20 minutes, stirring occasionally.

Cook fettuccine al denté. Add Velveeta cheese in small chunks and stir until cheese is melted. Add parmesan cheese, stir well. Add cooked fettuccine to mixture and stir until completely mixed together. Cover and remove from heat. Allow to stand for 5 minutes. Uncover and add green onion. Stir well. Serves 6-8.

❧ SHRIMP IN A CAJUN BUCKET ❧

½ LB	JUMBO SHRIMP	2 CUPS	ONION, CHOPPED
1 LB	GUMBO SHRIMP, VERY SMALL, PEELED	1 CUP	CELERY, CHOPPED
½ CUP	LUMP CRABMEAT	3 TBSP	GARLIC, MINCED
1 TBSP	CORN STARCH	¼ CUP	FRESH PARSLEY, CHOPPED
2 CUPS	HEAVY CREAM	1 TBSP	FLOUR
½ LB	FETTUCCINI, UNCOOKED	½ CUP	FRESH GREEN ONION, CHOPPED
¼ LB.	BUTTER		

Peel jumbo shrimp (reserve peeling) leaving last rib with tail attached. Rinse small shrimp and reserve. Preheat oven to 350°F. Cook fettuccine al denté. Carefully check lump crabmeat for any shell. To crabmeat, add corn starch and 1 tbsp. heavy cream and mix well. Place crabmeat equally in two ½ cup ramekin bowls that have been sprayed with vegetable spray.

Pat crabmeat down flat. Cover with foil, place in oven for 35 minutes. Next, place reserved shrimp shells into a 1-quart pot and add remaining heavy cream. Place on medium heat and stir well. As soon as cream begins to bubble, reduce heat to very low and stir frequently. In a large skillet melt butter. Add onion, celery, garlic and sauté until onions begin to wilt. Add parsley and stir well. Add jumbo shrimp and sauté until just cooked. Remove and set aside. Add small (gumbo) shrimp to skillet and stir well. Sauté until shrimp are pink. Add flour and stir in well. Strain heavy cream into skillet and stir in well. Bring to a rolling boil, reduce heat and stir well. Simmer 10 minutes, remove from heat. Add green onion and stir in well. Place pasta into 2 serving bowls or soup plates, remove crabmeat from ramekins and place in center of pasta. Press the middle of crabmeat gently until a pocket is formed. Arrange jumbo shrimp around crabmeat, hanging tail into pasta. Spoon cream mixture around the ends of the shrimp and in the center of the buckets. Garnish with a sprig of parsley and serve. Serves two.

❧ TROUT SUPREME ❧

¼ LB.	BUTTER
1 CUPS	ONION, CHOPPED
2 TBSP	GARLIC, MINCED
¼ CUP	FRESH PARSLEY, CHOPPED
½ CUP	CANNED MUSHROOMS, SLICED
1 LB	SHRIMP, PEELED AND DEVEINED
1 LB	LUMP CRABMEAT, CHECK CAREFULLY FOR SHELLS
2 CUPS	BREAD CRUMBS
¼-½ CUP	WATER
6	TROUT FILLETS, SKINNED
½ CUP	SEASONED BREAD CRUMBS
2	LEMONS

In a skillet melt butter. Add onion, garlic, parsley and simmer on medium heat for 5 minutes. Add mushrooms, shrimp and cook 10 more minutes. Add crabmeat and stir in until mixed well. Add 2 cups bread crumbs until you have a dry consistency. Add water to moisten enough to be patted into a ball. Let cool 1 hour. On a greased broiling pan, place trout fillets, skinned side down. Cover with crab mixture from end to end, about 1 inch thick. Sprinkle with seasoned bread crumbs and lemon. Cover with foil.

Bake for 10 minutes in a preheated 350°F oven. Remove and put oven on broil. Place pan in broiler for 2-3 minutes or until top browns as you like it. Good stuff!!!

CRAB BOIL

18-20 QTS	WATER	3 TBSP	BLACK PEPPER
2 CUPS	ONIONS, QUARTERED	3	LEMONS, QUARTERED
5 CLOVES	GARLIC	24	LIVE CRABS, THE LAKE VARIETY
2 PACKS	CRAB BOIL	¼ CUP	SALT
3 TBSP	CAYENNE PEPPER		

Fill a 28-quart pot to about ⅔ of capacity with water. Heat until a rolling boil. (Note: Use an outside boiler for best results but not required). Next, add onion, garlic, crab boil, cayenne, black pepper and lemons. Bring back to a rolling boil. Add crabs. Boil 15 minutes. Remove from heat, add salt, stir and let stand for 5 minutes, drain and eat..!!

⁓ Cajun Seasoning ⁓

Creole/Cajun Seasoning..128
Creole Seafood Seasoning..129
Creole/Cajun Vegetable Seasoning...130
Blackened Seasoning for Chicken...131
Blackened Seasoning for Fish...132
Blackened Seasoning for Beef...133
Your Own Blend of Seasoning...134

∾ Equivalent Chart ∾

3 TSP	1 TBSP
2 TBSP	⅛ CUP
4 TBSP	¼ CUP
8 TBSP	½ CUP
16 TBSP	1 CUP
5 TBSP + 1 TSP	⅓ CUP
12 TBSP	¾ CUP
4 OZ	½ CUP
8 OZ	1 CUP
16 OZ	1 LB
1 OZ	2 TBSP, FAT OR LIQUID
2 CUP	1 PINT
2 PINT	1 QUART
1 QUART	4 CUP
⅝ CUP	½ CUP + 2 TBSP
⅞ CUP	¾ CUP + 2 TBSP
1 JIGGER	1½ FL. OZ. (3 TBSP)
8 TO 10 EGG WHITES	1 CUP
12 TO 14 EGG YOLKS	1 CUP
1 CUP UNWHIPPED CREAM	2 CUP WHIPPED CREAM
1 LB. SHREDDED AMERICAN CHEESE	4 CUPS
¼ LB. CRUMBLED BLEU CHEESE	1 CUP
1 LEMON	3 TBSP JUICE
1 ORANGE	⅓ CUP JUICE
1 LB UNSHELLED WALNUTS	1½ TO 1¾ CUP SHELLED
2 CUPS FAT	1 LB
1 LB. BUTTER	2 CUPS OR 4 STICKS
2 CUPS GRANULATED SUGAR	1 LB
3½-4 CUPS UNSIFTED POWDERED SUGAR	1 LB
2¼ CUPS PACKED BROWN SUGAR	1 LB
4 CUPS SIFTED FLOUR	1 LB
4½ CUPS CAKE FLOUR	1 LB
3½ CUPS UNSIFTED WHOLE WHEAT FLOUR	1 LB
4 OZ. (1-1¼ CUPS) UNCOOKED MACARONI	2¼ CUP COOKED
7 OZ. SPAGHETTI	4 CUP COOKED
4 OZ. (1½ TO 2 CUPS) UNCOOKED NOODLES	2 CUPS COOKED
28 SALTINE CRACKERS	1 CUP CRUMBS
4 SLICES BREAD	1 CUP CRUMBS
14 SQUARE GRAHAM CRACKERS	1 CUP CRUMBS
22 VANILLA WAFERS	1 CUP CRUMBS

THIS CREOLE/CAJUN SEASONING SECTION is designed to help you to blend your own Creole/Cajun seasonings. You are free to experiment with the different blends to satisfy your own taste. In fact, there is a guideline for your own blend of seasoning later in this section. You will certainly find many different blends of Creole/Cajun seasoning on the market. In fact, no two blends are the same. Seasoning blends are basically the tastes of the blender. There is no right or wrong in blending seasonings. What really matters is the blend that works for you. This book offers my blends (or at least one version of each recipe.) All these blends are tried and proven to consistently season your food the "New Orleans" way. It will also improve your knowledge of cooking New Orleans style.

CREOLE/CAJUN SEASONING

USE ONLY DRIED SEASONINGS

1 CUP	SALT	½ CUP	GRANULATED GARLIC
2 TBSP	CAYENNE PEPPER	¼ CUP	ONION POWDER
¼ CUP	BLACK PEPPER	1½ TBSP	CELERY SEED

In a food processor add salt and cayenne pepper. Process for 30 seconds. Add black pepper, granulated garlic and process another 15 seconds. Add remaining ingredients and process another minute. Store in air-tight container. Use for gumbo, jambalaya, etouffée or for your regular cooking. You can also use like salt at the dinner table. Makes about 2¼ cups.

✑ Creole Seafood Seasoning ✑

Use only Dried Seasonings

1 CUP	Salt	¼ CUP	Granulated Garlic
½ CUP	Whole Sweet Basil	½ CUP	Onion Powder
2 TBSP	Cayenne Pepper	¼ CUP	Whole Thyme
¼ CUP	Black Pepper		

In a food processor add salt and whole sweet basil. Blend until color is evenly distributed. Next, add granulated garlic and cayenne pepper. Process another 30 seconds. Add remaining ingredients and blend 1 minute. You can use this in all stages of cooking. Sprinkle on top of baked or broiled fish—use in pot cooking or use at the dinner table. Makes 3 cups.

⤸ Creole/Cajun Vegetable Seasoning ⤷

Use only Dried Seasonings

1 cup	Salt	½ cup	Parsley Flakes
1 cup	White Pepper	1½ tbsp	Garlic Powder
¼ cup	Cayenne Pepper	¼ cup	Onion Powder
¼ cup	Black Pepper	¼ cup	Curry Powder

Put all ingredients in a food processor and blend for 2 minutes. Use in cooking or at the dinner table. Good for all types of vegetables, especially steamed. Makes almost 3½ cups.

✎ BLACKENED SEASONING FOR CHICKEN ✎

USE ONLY DRIED SEASONINGS

½ CUP	CAYENNE PEPPER
1 CUP	WHOLE OREGANO
½ CUP	WHOLE THYME
¼ CUP	SALT
½ CUP	BLACK PEPPER
½ CUP	PAPRIKA

In a food processor blend cayenne pepper, whole oregano and whole thyme for 1 minute. Add remaining ingredients and blend for another minute. Blackened seasoning is used to coat the chicken and fry in very hot butter for a short period of time. Follow your recipe instructions. This is not a good table seasoning. Makes 3¼ cups.

❧ Blackened Seasoning for Fish ❧

Use only Dried Seasonings
½ CUP	CAYENNE PEPPER
1 CUP	WHOLE OREGANO
½ CUP	WHOLE THYME
1 TBSP	SALT
1 TBSP	BLACK PEPPER

In a food processor blend cayenne pepper, whole oregano and whole thyme for 1 minute. Add remaining ingredients and process for another minute. Blackened seasoning is used to coat the fish and fry in very hot butter for a short period of time. Follow your recipe instructions. This is not a good table seasoning. Makes 2 cups + 2 tbsp.

✎ BLACKENED SEASONING FOR BEEF ✐

USE ONLY DRIED SEASONINGS

½ CUP	CAYENNE PEPPER
½ CUP	WHOLE OREGANO
¼ CUP	CRUSHED ROSEMARY
½ CUP	PAPRIKA
¼ CUP	SALT
¼ CUP	BLACK PEPPER

In a food processor blend cayenne pepper, whole oregano and crushed rosemary for 1 minute. Add remaining ingredients and process for another minute. Blackened seasoning is used to coat the meat and fry in very hot butter for a short period of time. Follow your recipe instructions. This is not a good table seasoning. Makes 2½ cups.

❧ Your Own Blend of Seasoning ❧

Making your own seasoning blend is really very simple if you give some thought to your cooking habits and techniques. First thing is to go to your seasoning rack or shelf and remove your most used seasonings. Next place the seasonings that you use in everything (or almost everything) on the side. If you think about it, you will find that you use these seasonings in the same proportion in virtually everything you cook. Measure out the amounts of these seasonings as you normally use them. If you don't usually measure, then you need to pay attention to the amounts of each seasoning that you use. Write it down each time you cook, and make sure that the ratio of seasonings is consistent each time you use them. Once you have established the seasonings you use, in the amounts and ratio you use them, you can begin to blend. Use the seasoning chart to help you mix.

1 TSP	x 3	=	1 TBSP
1 TBSP	x 4	=	¼ CUP
¼ CUP	x 4	=	1 CUP
1 CUP	x 4	=	1 QUART

When you have established the ratios of dry seasonings that you use, it is easy to make your blend. In a food processor add all the ingredients in the proper amounts and blend for 1 to 2 minutes, or until you are satisfied. To use your dry seasoning blend, compile the amount of each of the dry seasonings that you use in cooking. Add those amounts together and use that much of the blend.

135

(CONTINUES)

EXAMPLE: You have established the cooking ratios of your favorite dry seasonings to be the following:

1 TBSP	SALT	1 TBSP	ONION POWDER
1 TSP	BLACK PEPPER	2 TBSP	PARSLEY FLAKES
1 TBSP	GRANULATED GARLIC	2 TBSP	WHOLE SWEET BASIL

Now that you know the amounts and ratios of the dry seasonings that you use most, you can make your blend. For this example, say you want to blend enough to make 10 average recipes. Simply multiply the ingredients times 10.

1 TBSP SALT	X 10	=	10 TBSP	=	½ CUP + 2 TBSP
1 TSP BLACK PEPPER	X 10	=	10 TSP	=	3 TBSP + 1 TSP
1 TBSP GRANULATED GARLIC	X 10	=	10 TBSP	=	½ CUP + 2 TBSP
1 TBSP ONION POWDER	X 10	=	10 TBSP	=	½ CUP + 2 TBSP
2 TBSP PARSLEY FLAKES	X 10	=	20 TBSP	=	1+¼ CUPS
2 TBSP WHOLE SWEET BASIL	X 10	=	20 TBSP	=	1+¼ CUPS

Now that you know the proper amounts to blend, your recipe is as follows:

½ CUP + 2 TBSP	SALT
3 TBSP + 1 TSP	BLACK PEPPER
½ CUP + 2 TBSP	GRANULATED GARLIC
½ CUP + 2 TBSP	ONION POWDER
1+¼ CUPS	PARSLEY FLAKES
1+¼ CUPS	WHOLE SWEET BASIL

Place all ingredients in a food processor and blend for 1 to 2 minutes until all ingredients are totally blended. Note: the dry leafy ingredients will reduce in measurement by ½ when totally blended. When using the seasoning blend, take this into consideration.

(CONTINUES)

EXAMPLE: Your originally established example seasoning recipe.

1 TBSP	SALT
1 TSP	BLACK PEPPER
1 TBSP	GRANULATED GARLIC
1 TBSP	ONION POWDER
2 TBSP	PARSLEY FLAKES (1 TBSP PROCESSED)
2 TBSP	WHOLE SWEET BASIL (1 TBSP PROCESSED)

Add all ingredients to establish the total to use in each recipe. In this example the total is 5 tbsp + 1 tsp (80ml). (Remember that the dry leafy ingredients were cut by ½ to measure actual mass.)

Per Use Amount:

5 TBSP + 1 TSP $=$ ¼ CUP + 1 TBSP + 1 TSP

Remember that recipes will call for different amounts of seasoning according to quantities of food cooked. When deciding how much to use in that recipe, adjust the amount of the blend you use by the amount of salt you would use and that will give you the proper amount for all the other ingredients in the blend. For instance, if you would use 1 tbsp salt then use the established per use amount. If you use 2 tbsp of salt, then double the established per use amount, etc.

Note: Don't forget to write down the recipe for your blend. File it where you can find it for future blending.

∽ Louisiana Products ∾

Wherever I go to demonstrate cooking, I am constantly asked for information about ordering Louisiana products once the out-of-state (or country) buyer gets home. It also occurred to me that many people are receiving this book as a gift or are buying without meeting someone who can give information about Louisiana products to them. If you write to me and provide your mailing address, I will be happy to provide you with Louisiana businesses that carry meats, spices and gifts. The listing is adequate to provide you with sources of quality, hard-to-get products from our fair state.

If you have received this book as a gift, have ordered from me directly, or purchased this book out of Louisiana, and are having trouble getting the information that you want, then don't hesitate to write to me.

If you are interested in getting on my mailing list, then just drop me a letter requesting it and send to:

Remy Laterrade
P.O. Box 3942
Lafayette, LA 70502-3942

If you haven't had a chance to visit Louisiana, then I invite you to enjoy our "food, folks and fun," as well as the finest place in the country for architecture and other great sights. The plantations, the theme parks, the music, food and culture are all here for you to come and enjoy. While you are making your plans to visit us, then please consider visiting Lafayette. We are located on I-10 exit #'s 100, 101 and 103.

YA'LL COME!

⟋ ORDER MORE BOOKS NOW!!! ⟍

I have more cookbooks in stock now! If you are having problems getting extra copies of *"Dat Little Cajun Cookbook,"* *"Dat Little New Orleans Creole Cookbook,"*, *"Dat Little Out Of The Ordinary Cookbook,"* *"Dat Little New Orleans Plantation Cookbook,"* *"Dat Little Low Sugar Cajun Cookbook,"* or you want to get a copy of my first cookbook, *"I Want 'Dat Cajun Cookbook,"* then use the other side of this page to order more books.

Ordering is easy…just fill out your name and "UPS" shipping address as well as your "mailing" address. Please give your phone number, should there be any problems. Fill out how many books you want and add prices according to instructions. Be sure to add shipping and handling as directed.

Mail to the address given; allow 4-6 weeks for delivery.

SHIP TO: NAME_____   _____

UPS ADDRESS_____

CITY _____STATE _____ZIP _____

MAILING ADDRESS_____

CITY _____STATE _____ZIP _____

PHONE _____

❏ PLEASE ADD MY NAME TO YOUR MAILING LIST

Make Checks Payable to:
Remy Laterrade • P.O. Box 3942 • Lafayette, LA 70502 • Do Not Send Cash!

		QUANTITY	TOTAL
I Want 'Dat Cajun Cookbook by Remy	First Copy, $18.95	_____	_____
	Each Additional Copy $17.95		
'Dat Little New Orleans Creole Cookbook by Remy	Each Copy, $7.95	_____	_____
'Dat Little Cajun Cookbook by Remy	Each Copy, $7.95	_____	_____
'Dat Little Louisiana Plantation Cookbook by Remy	Each Copy, $7.95	_____	_____
'Dat Little Out Of The Ordinary Cookbook by Remy	Each Copy, $7.95	_____	_____
'Dat Little Low-Sugar Cajun Cookbook by Remy	Each Copy, $7.95	_____	_____
	Shipping and Handling, First Book, $2.50		$ 2.50
	Shipping and Handling, Each Additional Book, $1.50	_____	_____
		TOTAL	_____

SHIP TO:

NAME_____

UPS ADDRESS_____

CITY _____ STATE _____ ZIP _____

MAILING ADDRESS_____

CITY _____ STATE _____ ZIP _____

PHONE_____

Make Checks Payable to: Remy Laterrade • P.O. Box 3942 • Lafayette, LA 70502 • Do Not Send Cash!